Leaning Into Six Sigma

The path to integration of
Lean Enterprise and Six Sigma

Barbara Wheat, Chuck Mills, and Mike Carnell

Publishing Partners
Boulder City, Nevada

Published by Publishing Partners
1400 Colorado Street, Boulder City, Nevada 89005
E-mail PublishBooks@aol.com

Printed in the United States of America

Acknowledgements

The authors would like to thank Nick and Terry Russell at Publishing Partners for their help in publishing this book. Nick, for his expertise in navigating the rough waters of the publishing world, and Terry for her diligent proofreading.

Thank you,
Barbara, Chuck, and Mike

Foreword for
Leaning Into Six Sigma

After reading the manuscript, *Leaning Into Six Sigma* I enthusiastically agreed to contribute the foreword when Mike Carnell asked me.

The Six Sigma concept and Total Cycle Time (Lean Enterprise), were two of the Key Initiatives originated at Motorola back in the mid-1980s which I was fortunate enough to be a part of. This Continuous Improvement methodology works, as evidenced by the fact that many companies and quality consultants today are deploying it and are expounding remarkable bottom line $$$ savings when deploying it correctly. Even the worldwide organization of the American Society for Quality will be establishing a new certification exam for Six Sigma Black Belts, which truly demonstrates how institutionalized the Six Sigma processes have become.

This is the type of book you want every company employee, especially the executive leaders and middle management, to read before you start into your Lean/Six Sigma deployment. Everyone effects change in an organization and can relate to the various characters and their roles in this book, including the administrative assistant Celia.

The authors have done an excellent job explaining in a non-technical way the Six Sigma problem solving methodology MAIC (Measure, Analyze, Improve and Control), and why it is critical that it be linked to the 5S's of Lean Enterprise.

This modern day fable, which can be read on your next short flight, depicts the "typical company" looking for a quick fix to improve a major chronic quality and month end delivery bottleneck, which is band-aided with significant overtime, and results in poor financials. Sam "that guy, the consultant," is invited to visit Sid the Plant Owner to help him make the decision on what machine to buy. Sam runs into a typical "Crows Nest" everywhere she looks in the company. You have your Doubting Thomas (the Manufacturing Supervisor, George), who has been there since the doors opened and helped Sid to build the business to what it is today.

As they work with the "problem child department team" using the 5S's and deploying MAIC problem solving methodology, both Sid and George realize things need to change, and become real advocates and Champions for change.

An exit strategy for Sam is developed, so that the ownership of the new problem solving methodologies are internalized and institutionalized by the company's leadership and staff. The end comes so quickly you are left wondering what happens next, when will the second book come out, explaining how or what will be the company's next Breakthrough Strategy? I'm sure some of us know the answer!!!

I strongly urge anyone who is thinking of deploying the Lean/Six Sigma methodology to read this book. Based on the "real life" comments and examples used, it is evident the authors have lived what they are preaching, successfully deploying Lean/Six Sigma in all types of applications, including manufacturing, service industries, financial institutions, government, research and design, development, aerospace, etc.

The book captures the true spirit of Six Sigma and Continuous Improvement which made Motorola great, and I am sure it will be appreciated by many of the early pioneers of Six Sigma.

John A. Lupienski, Motorola, Inc.

The Lean Enterprise is based on the understanding that work is a system of inputs resulting in an output of value.
The inputs are transformed with the premise that anywhere work is being done, waste is being generated.
The Lean Enterprise seeks to organize its processes to the optimum level, through the continual focus on the identification and elimination of waste.

- Barbara Wheat -

Chapter One

On Becoming *That Guy*

I'm that guy. I haven't always been that guy. It is a relatively new position for me. Only over the past 3 years have I joined the ranks of this club of "that guys." You know who we are, the ones your boss hires to help you address issues in your organization that you already know the solution to. Yep, that's me, one of those damned consultant guys. No matter that I'm a female, consultant guys are gender neutral.

The interesting part of being in this club is the polarized impression people tend to have toward us, they either hate us or love us. Unfortunately, the general population's perception of the entire club is generally based on the limited interaction they have with one or two members. Hey, I know how it is. Some "guy" comes into your organization, asks a bunch of questions and then puts your responses into a nicely packaged format and finally gives you a deliverable that is a mirror image of your own solution to your problem.

So why the hell do you pay for information you already have? Lets start this examination of the issue with a personal example of the phenomenon. I work primarily in the manufacturing world. In fact my non-formal title is "plant rat." Clients and colleagues have given me that title and I am quite proud of it. I am one of those very odd individuals who loves the "real" problems that only a factory can provide.

Now let's talk about why consultants leave the "real world" to become one of "those guys." I was actually very happy with my last professional employer, working as part of a team to solve chronic problems in our organization. The problems are actually the easiest part of my job. Solving those problems requires science, the problem costs money, and the organization is financially driven, so the assumption would be that the support required to solve the problem would be a no-brainer, right? Yeah, right!

Every step toward implementing the solution for this chronic problem is an exercise in trial by fire. A political minefield that leaves you wondering what could have possessed you to walk blindly into the issues without a structured map showing where the "mines" are and how to avoid them. But luckily (or so you would think) you live through the politics, you fix the problem, and while you don't get a rousing rendition of *Pomp and Circumstance* for meeting the challenge, you do get the satisfaction of a job well done. You expect that even more importantly, you have finally earned that thing. You know, that "credibility" thing that everyone is always searching for but rarely finds.

You just know that you have met your objective this time. Finally, after more times than you can count, you have proven yourself to the point that you will no longer need to fight these political battles to solve the next problem. You finally made it. Of course it comes as a complete surprise that the rest of the organization just doesn't quite see the situation the same way that you do. Various compilations of the statement "you're almost there kid, don't give up now," pop into your head as you stroll toward your boss's office to turn in your resignation.

But this time, you've had it. This time you decide that you're tired of fighting for what you know is right and you are ready to join an organization that recognizes your problem solving skills, where politics take a back seat to business decisions. As you walk out the door, your boss is telling you what a huge mistake you are making.

When the interviewing begins, you find that your boss was right. No matter who you talk to, there is a definite political force in the organization that leads to poor business decisions made for political reasons. At that point, you decide you'll fight this tendency on your own. Hang out your CONSULTANT shingle and get started.

What a naive little soul. By the time you have joined the ranks of the "one of those guys" club, it has become so contaminated that being a consultant is almost as bad as being a lawyer, relative to the number of "bottom feeder" jokes flying around the business world. But, here you are. So you vow to be the best darn consultant ever. No shades of gray here, only black and white, good and bad, yes it's right or no it's wrong. No "little white lies" for you.

Things go pretty good for a while, you manage to build up a strong relationship with your clients, and very soon you have more business that you can deliver on. Not too bad a position to be in. What happens next is particularly amusing. Remember the company you were working for before you took out on your own? Well, one day you get a call from your old boss. Seems the company has come up against a problem they can't solve, and they would like to hire you to consult with them for a solution.

Leaning Into Six Sigma

Can you believe this? At $65K per year as an employee, you had to scratch, fight, and fend for yourself, and now at $3K per day, they are willing to step up to any solution you propose as though it was an epiphany from above! You can't help but wonder, *"What is wrong with this picture?"* But, you know what the problem is and how best to solve it, so you go about things in the same manner as before you left the organization, and solve the problem without the political constraints, reaching conclusion in about 1/10th of the time it took before. Surprised?

Then you run into that client, the one who knows they have a problem, but they have no idea where or what the problem is. You go through the process of determining the root cause, and plan the strategy for containing and then eliminating the problem. But the client does not want to go through the process. They are not happy with the solution because it involves more cultural buy-in than they want to commit to. In other words, they want the easy fix.

Well, easy fixes sometimes cause more problems than they solve! There are the finger in the dike, stop-gap fixes; cut costs, reorganize (again), and your classic of classics, firefighting. But all that's happening here is that you're greasing the squeaking wheel. You may realize some short-term improvements in specific areas, but usually these gains are at the expense of some other operation that will surface later.

A few months back a gentleman, Sid Glick of SG, Inc., called my office and asked if I would have lunch with him to discuss a problem he was having at his plant. "Sam," he said (that's me, Sam Micawh), "I'm considering the purchase of a new five axis CNC machine to the tune of a million-two, or

4

a four axis for three quarters of a million dollars. I would like you to evaluate my backlog, part configurations, and run rates on these machines, and help me to determine which would be the smarter buy."

Well, this was refreshing! A person who had apparently done his homework, determined the root cause of his capacity problem, and has the solution narrowed to two options. I agreed to meet with Sid the following Tuesday for lunch. I should have known it wasn't going to be that easy.

We met on Tuesday, as agreed, at Sid's favorite home cooking café. After the usual pleasantries, Sid blurted, "I called you because you were highly recommended by some colleagues of mine who told me you knew your stuff. So give me your best guess, the five or the four?"

I told Sid I would rather not guess, but I would like to look at the plant and review the data that brought him to the five axis or four axis decision. Sid told me he would be glad to show me through the plant, but there was no specific data that prompted his choices. He said he would introduce me to George, the plant supervisor, who has been working at SG, Inc. for 26 years. "George is the one that told me if we were going to reduce our backlog and start meeting delivery schedules we needed a new machine."

"*Oops!*," was the first thought that popped into my mind. "*SG, Inc. is about to make a million dollar capital expenditure decision based on "tribal knowledge" and no data to substantiate the decision.*" My lunch suddenly became unsettled, so as we were checking out, I bought some antacids and we started to the plant.

Leaning Into Six Sigma

Chapter Two

The Plant, My First Impressions

As we drove up to the plant my first thought was that Sid had done a mighty good job picking out his location. Instead of one single building, SG actually consisted of two moderately sized structures that were situated side by side. The two facilities were joined by a paved walkway that had trees and shrubs planted alongside them to mark the pathway between locations, and there were people strolling back and forth. The landscaping was nicely manicured and reminded me more of a park than a manufacturing facility. The buildings were clean and the lawns manicured. In the back of my mind I was thinking *"OK, I could spend a week or two working in this environment."*

As Sid motioned me into the visitors parking area, I thought I caught sight of something that might be a problem, but I decided to reserve my personal thoughts until I saw the rest of the plant. Still… In the back of my mind I had this nagging thought, *"Why would an organization this small need to have all those tractor trailers parked back there? There's no way they can be moving that much material in and out of this place..."*

As soon as we hit the front door, a small middle aged woman in a snappy business suit met Sid. Before I was even introduced it became apparent that this was his secretary. I knew I'd better get in good with this woman, because I have found over the past few years that plant managers (or business owners, for that matter) think they run the place, but the secretaries are the ones who really keep things going. If I wanted to do any type of business with Sid, I'd better make sure this woman liked me. In order to make sure, I slapped on my best smile and extended my hand to introduce myself.

" Hello, my name is Sam," I said, "and who might you be?"

The no nonsense look she gave me said she wasn't going to decide she liked me just because I smiled and took the initiative to introduce myself, and within the blink of an eye, her words confirmed what her look suggested. "Well, I *might* be Joan of Ark" she said without the slightest hint of a smile, "but I *am* Celia Gordon. I'm Sid's executive administrative assistant".

"Oh, shit!" was the first thought that went through my mind, and it didn't change as I shook her icy hand for the quickest handshake I've ever (not) enjoyed. Luckily, she was in a hurry and scurried away without even a whisper of goodbye.

Sid just looked at me and shrugged, "She's always like that. Just ignore it and she'll warm up to you." I didn't say a word, but what I wanted to tell him was that it would take a bottle of acetylene and a blowtorch to warm that woman up, and I'm not sure there's a bottle of acetylene that big in the world. But I didn't say a word, just stood there and smiled - weakly.

As we walked toward Sid's office, George was the next person we ran into. Sid introduced us, and then quickly pointed out that this was the same George he had mentioned in the restaurant, the same George that told him to buy the new piece of equipment. George shook my hand and said "Pleased 'ta meet ya....." as we continued to walk toward Sid's office. As we sat across the table from each other, George began telling me the history of Sid's business and his pride in the fact that he was one of only a handful of people left in the company that had been there since the very beginning.

As George went through the history of SG, I realized that he had a good reason to be proud. Over a 30 year time frame, the company had grown from two guys machining parts to an organization with over 500 full time employees and more than $300 million in sales annually. They were well respected in their industry, although recent quality concerns and late delivery issues were causing problems with some of their biggest contracted customers. These problems could be fixed with the new equipment. George had no doubt about that, and I certainly wasn't going to say otherwise. At least not yet.

As George wrapped up his history lesson, Sid suggested that I might like to see the facility. George was between production meetings and said he would be happy to show me the plant. As we walked into the facility I had mixed emotions. The consultant part of me was screaming at all the things I saw wrong, and I had an immediate urge to point out everything to George as we passed by; but the (semi) human side of me screamed that this would be wrong. Just looking at and listening to him as he showed me the various processes they had established throughout the plant, it was pretty obvious that if I said too much too soon, I'd find myself on my butt in a minute. Since George was quite a bit bigger than me, I decided to listen to my human side. For a change.

One thing that I couldn't be quiet about though, and decided to confirm by asking George, was the level of hostility I sensed in the plant as we walked through. In several areas as we passed, the operators started banging their tools on work benches and tables in an apparent protest of my being in the plant. In other areas they just scowled at me, and I wasn't sure which I found more unsettling. I asked George if SG had some labor problems.

"Yep" he snickered. I decided to take the issue up with Sid later, after the tour.

When the plant tour was over, George led me back to Sid's office and shook my hand at the door. "I'm really glad you came to have a look at the place," he said. "Since he'll have the opinion of an outsider now, I guess he'll listen to me". As George walked away, I realized that he was telling me that when I gave Sid the same recommendation that he had, Sid would buckle and get the new equipment. Whoops, this was going to be a problem. I had no intention of giving Sid the opinion that he needed a new piece of equipment. Not yet anyway.

As I slowly opened the door to Sid's office, he motioned me to come in and have a seat. Sid was on the phone so I sat down and began looking around at the plaques on the wall.

Leaning Into Six Sigma

Several were from suppliers for outstanding quality and cost reduction and on time delivery, but none of the plaques had dates less than ten years old. Not a very good sign, but I didn't say a word, just made a mental note.

"Well, waddya think? Can I get by with the smaller piece of equipment, or should I just bite the bullet and go all out?" Sid spoke with such blatant pride that I almost didn't have the heart to tell him what I'd seen. Almost.

"You know Sid, it may be possible to increase your quality and capacity levels without buying new equipment. If you would like, I can take a few minutes to give you my impressions of the facility, and then we can talk about some less expensive ways to bring your quality up and your cycle time down using the equipment you already have."

Sid smiled, and said he liked the sound of that, so I asked him for a few minutes to get my thoughts together and write some notes. Sid said that was perfect because he had a meeting scheduled that should take about an hour. He asked Celia to find me a quiet space so I could work and said he'd meet me back in his office around 4:30 so we could talk.

Judging by our first greeting, I expected Celia to locate me in a cleaning closet filled with plenty of toxic chemicals somewhere, but instead she showed me to a small conference room with a desk and phone, and told me where the restrooms were, as well as the snack bar and smoking areas. A definite improvement from earlier that day and I even thought I saw a hint of a smile as she turned to leave. But it was probably just the light playing tricks on me.

When I sat down to collect my thoughts I realized that my impressions were even worse than I had consciously realized. Without the threat of George knocking me on my

11

butt, the truth of what I saw came out pretty freely and the truth was ugly. The word "ugly" stuck in my mind. I remembered when I first got started in consulting, a friend in the business told me that you never want to tell the customer they have an ugly baby. His not-so-charming way of saying that you don't bad mouth the customer's processes, or initiatives they have attempted to instill positive improvement. I tried to keep that in mind as I prepared my notes, but it wasn't easy. Sid had an ugly baby.

At exactly 4:30 I walked out of the conference room and headed toward Sid's office. About 20 feet from the door, George called from behind, "Hey Sam, wait up." He jogged the few steps between us and said "Hope you don't mind, but Sid asked me to join you." My mind started racing. How to position myself far enough between the two men as to insure that neither of them could reach me with a wide swing? I had to make sure they would have to charge me before they hit, and since they were both older, I hoped I was faster and could get through the door before they could reach me. Although George looked like he was in pretty good shape. I'd better put myself closer to the door, and maybe leave it open just a bit.

Sid was waiting and looked eager, so I began talking as soon as we had exchanged pleasantries. Now, sensitive I'm not! If I was, I would have noticed the look on the faces of both Sid and George as I waded deeper into my impressions of the facility. When I was finished running down my laundry list of things that were wrong, I looked up at them and was amazed by the shock in their eyes. I immediately looked down at the scribbled notes in my lap to see what I said that would be so devastating to the two men:

Leaning Into Six Sigma

- The plant is filthy
- There is no control of non-conforming parts
- There is no semblance of lot control for work in process or finished goods inventory
- Operators are performing their work sloppily and to no particular standard
- There is no apparent flow to the processes
- There is so much inventory in the plant that no one knows what they have and what they don't have
- The quality departments are trying mightily to inspect quality into the product
- There are excess and broken tooling and fixtures scattered everywhere in the plant
- The lighting is very poor and work conditions are unsafe
- All raw inventory is contaminated, and there is no sure method of controlling inventory. You have raw material stored line side that looks like it's been there for years
- Your material handlers are running all over the plant with nothing on their forklifts, wasting gas, polluting the air, and endangering each other and the process operator
- Your hazardous materials are not stored properly in the plant
- You have years of inventory on trailers out back (this is what I was afraid of when I parked earlier in the day)
- The few control charts you have scattered about the plant are outdated by months and no one is even looking at them - thank goodness

- Your processes are batch producing because your
  set up times are so long
- The last processes before final inspection are
  being starved for WIP for hours of each shift because
  of the batch and queue methods you're practicing
- People are standing all over the plant waiting for
  something to do

Uh oh, maybe I'd gone a little overboard! Sometimes I have a tendency to forget that I'm talking about someone's business when I give my impressions, and from the look on their faces, I may have just stepped over the line. I slowly moved my chair a little closer to the door; luckily the chair was on wheels. As an afterthought, I finished my onslaught with "Look at it this way, knowing there's a problem is half the battle."

Sid took a minute before he responded. I'm sure he was clenching and unclenching his fists under the desk while we waited. "Sam, I'm not sure you remember why I asked you here. I'm not looking for your opinion of the state of my company. I just wanted to know which piece of equipment I should purchase in order to make sure I meet my upcoming customer demands."

My response to this comment made my earlier litany look like child's play. I spoke once more without my 'fit human interaction filter' and said, "Look Sid, if you keep up the way you're going out there, you won't have any problems meeting your customer demands because you won't have any customers."

Before Sid could get in his next comment, I decided to finish my thoughts. I don't know exactly the words I used,

Leaning Into Six Sigma

but they were something to the effect that SG's quality had to be below one Sigma with all the things they were doing wrong, and that their inventory turns were a joke. That if they wanted to compete in today's market they were going to have to learn to be more efficient and focus on eliminating waste from all their processes. Because if their manufacturing processes were bad, I had to assume that their transactional processes were in even worse shape. I ended by telling them that of course we couldn't be sure, because everything was in such disarray that we couldn't even tell how bad things were, and the employees were so pissed off that they wouldn't tell you if the building was burning down.

George finally shook himself out of shock and said there was no way I could tell all those things from a brief 45 minute walk through the plant, and added that he should have known I would try to dig in and get paid my daily rate forever.

I conceded that George might be right about my quick assessment and proceeded to ask some basic questions:

1. What are your inventory turns?
2. What is your overall quality level?
3. Do you measure quality as a percentage or PPM level?
4. Do you final inspect every product you build?
5. How do you determine your inventory levels?
6. What does your PM schedule look like?
7. What is your OI?
8. Are your margins on some products negative?
9. Does your workforce understand the concept of waste?

10. When was the last employee suggestion for improvement made?
11. How often do you conduct a physical inventory?
12. What is the rate of over/under you typically see in inventory?

As George haltingly answered the few questions he could, a look of caution began to form on Sid's face. At the end of my interrogation, Sid looked at me and said, "I've heard about that Sigma stuff, and inventory turns, but I don't really know much about any of it. So what can I do?"

The answer I gave really surprised Sid, and I think it pissed him off as well. "We need to get organized out there. Just give me a week to work with one of your teams and we'll start a program of 5S in your facility. I'll teach them what 5S means and how it applies, then work with them to establish the principles in their work area. After that, we can select some of your more dedicated people and have them teach the technique across the organization."

At this George grinned from ear to ear, "Yeah, I'm gonna love seeing you try to get these guys to clean up their work area. There's no way in hell they'll ever do it! We can't even get them to walk to the trash can at lunch time, they just leave everything laying all over the snack bar for someone else to clean up." Then George explained how SG had to hire a clean up crew to go behind every shift and clean up after the employees in order to keep the health inspector off their case.

I gave George my 'I understand' nod and said, "Just give me the week, and tell me where you want to start. If I fail, you pay for one week and I'll be gone. If I succeed, you may just find that you increase your capacity and margins considerably without any capital expense, and that would be a good thing".

George started to argue, but Sid held up his hand and said "You've got a deal. Tell us which day you want to start, we'll have the training room set up and the people there for you. You have one week to make this 5S thing work, then we'll meet with the team you're training and discuss the results." George just shook his head and looked at the floor.

After giving Celia the date I wanted for the first session, and shaking Sid and George's hand, I walked out to the car for the drive home. It was already dark outside and I had a lot of planning and thinking to do. Some time soon I would have to have my head examined. I wasn't sure when I had developed this death wish, but I knew it wasn't healthy. No time for that now though, there was work to be done.

Leaning Into Six Sigma

Chapter Three

It's Just Housekeeping
(With a little furniture moving thrown in)

On the appointed Monday morning, I arrived at the factory ready for confrontation; in fact I was prepared for several confrontations. I walked into the training center guided by Celia and began setting the room up for the week's training. I had planned on conducting the workshop as five - 8 hour sessions, in which two of the days would be used working on the actual workplace changes. I would start the class with some introductions, and then begin the training with a discussion on the identification and elimination of waste.

As class participants began to arrive, I realized that my planning was a joke. The first person arrived and plopped down in his seat, simultaneously throwing his clipboard across the table in front of him. I tried to shake his hand, but he just grunted and turned away. This behavior was repeated several times over the next few minutes until I had a total of ten sullen people sitting before me with a look on their faces somewhere between anger and pity. Okay, so much for structured classroom interaction. There was no way I could direct these people until they said what was on their minds.

I began the session by introducing myself and telling some really lame jokes. Next, I asked them to take a few minutes to talk with each other and find out something new about each of the people in the room. They started off slowly, but before too long they were talking quite candidly between each other, and grew pretty animated when they were discussing anything other than SG.

Of course, every time I tried to join the conversations, they clammed up. I eventually got wise enough to sit on a table at the front of the room observing, and keep my mouth shut.

After about an hour of classroom interaction, I asked if anyone needed a smoke break. More than half of the class growled "yeah" at me, so I told them to take fifteen minutes, and then we'd get started. Nearly thirty minutes later I finally got everyone back into the room and started trying to get them to talk. My first few attempts didn't go very well and I was starting to feel pretty frustrated. Before long I was feeling sweat run down my back and I could hear my voice start to quiver. These people were more than upset, they were down right pissed off! It didn't help me to hear them whisper about sugar in gas tanks and slashed tires.

The only woman in the group finally took pity on me and stood up to discuss what she had found out about her fellow classmates. She introduced one young man and explained that he was the cherry pit spitting champion of his county. It was comic, but broke the ice for the rest of the group, or at least cracked it a little.

Leaning Into Six Sigma

It was mostly nerves I suppose, but I found myself laughing (a little too much) and suddenly very interested in the sport of spitting cherry pits. By the end of the introductions we were a little more relaxed, but not to the point I had hoped for. We spent more time on smoke breaks than working the first half of the day, but since the class appeared to be as uncomfortable as I was, I decided to let it slide. Just after lunch I noticed Sid ducking into the back of the room. I acted like I didn't see him there and just kept moving through the material, hoping to increase the discussion between members of the class. They were completely shut down while Sid was in the room and he just sat and shook his head. I got the impression he was thinking he knew this wouldn't work, and more importantly, I figured he was probably right.

After he left the room the class noticeably relaxed and I said, "Man, that sucked." The group took a double take at me and asked what I was talking about. Most of the participants had no idea who Sid was, they had never even met him. I jumped at the chance to tell them that I figured Sid would be calling off the class tomorrow because the session seemed to be going nowhere. I also explained to them that I had been asked to help out because Sid realized that most of their processes sucked. The group acted shocked to hear this. The same outgoing woman who had spoken up earlier, Michelle, said "You mean he knows how bad things are getting here? We didn't think he had a clue!"

I explained the concerns I had discussed with Sid on my first visit to the facility, and that he had agreed to allow me into the facility for one week to see if I could make a difference. I also told them that Sid was convinced that the

21

workforce would not be willing to work to make the changes.

For a split second, I was pretty sure they were about to kill me. Then they opened up in a flood of conversation. "Why should we help? What are we supposed to do? How will this help us?" and on and on... I spent the rest of the day discussing what was possible and giving examples of how we could improve their processes.

I explained the seven elements of waste. Overproduction, correction, inventory, processing, motion, conveyance, and waiting, and how to identify them in the workplace. They spent about a half hour listing examples of each of the elements in their own work process, a total of 21 examples of areas where they could eliminate excess from the process. I also spent some time talking about workplace organization, introducing the 5S's

- Sifting
- Sorting
- Sweeping and Washing
- Spic and Span
- Self-discipline

We discussed how the 5S process would improve safety and workflow and allow them to better manage the process as a whole. We also discussed how we could reduce the costs associated with the rework caused by not controlling the process inputs.

As we went deeper into this discussion they opened up and provided one idea after another on how to improve their work area. The group agreed to start the next morning's session by touring their work area and teaching me the process as it was currently performed. In the last fifteen minutes of the day, Sid ducked back in to the room and listened. As the class filed out, they passed Sid with quiet greetings and reserved smiles.

Sid looked like he was in shock as he turned to me and asked "What did you do, drug those guys?"

I smiled and said "Nope, I just talked to them, and more importantly, I listened."

We started the next day's session at 7 A.M. on the factory floor. The group took about an hour to show me the process and how the work flowed through the area, or more specifically, how the work didn't flow. As I went around reading inventory tags on the raw materials I was surprised to see dates going back over five years. There was so much inventory it was impossible to determine what was needed in their actual process. There were spare tools and fixtures everywhere and nothing seemed to be attached to any particular area in the process.

The process was fed by work-in-process from a subassembly area located across the aisle. The subassembly operators had produced so much excess inventory that they had actually built a 'wall of inventory' around their work area. As we continued to tour the main work area, the subassembly process operators came across the aisle and asked what we were doing. I stepped aside and allowed the operators on the main line to explain what they had learned, and I was surprised to hear them repeat what I had told them during the previous afternoon. It wasn't just that they had listened to what I taught them, but that they were actually excited about what they were going to do in their process.

The guys from the subassembly process started talking about what they could do to bring their process into the main line. This move would allow them to build just what was needed to keep the main line running. The savings for this move and reduction of work in process inventory would more than pay for the class we were holding that week, including all the resources required (*and my fees*).

It was hard to rein the team in to the point where we could get them back into the classroom. They were so revved up that they wanted to get started right away. I asked them to bear with me and we went back to the class to begin our plan for the next two days.

I started the next session by explaining Dr. Deming's P-D-C-A cycle and making sure they understood the importance of *Planning* in the cycle. After some arguing and further discussion, they agreed that we needed to plan for success or we would end up not getting the job completed. We first listed everything that had to be done and the time allotted (which was 2½ days). The first task at hand was the *Sifting* process. We needed to check everything in the work area and remove everything that was not required to do the job. Next we would look at the flow of work, and organize the tools and component items in such a way as to insure safety and reduce walk and wait time in the process.

The team had some excellent ideas, and once again I found myself trying to calm them down long enough to finish the planning.

Next, we planned for the *Sorting* of items. Each operator would be responsible for defining the location for their tools and equipment. All team members would provide their input, but in the final decision we would look to the process operator.

Lastly, the team would clean every surface in the work

area, and label all the items for semi-permanent storage. The goal of the 5S process would be the ability to identify what was required in the work process, and if anything was missing *AT A GLANCE* !!!

Believe it or not, they were jazzed! After class, my pal Michelle stayed to tell me that she hadn't seen her fellow employees this excited in over 10 years. They had apparently just given up. As the pressures of the business increased and the company grew, Sid had stopped listening to all but a few of his supervisors and subsequently the employees stopped talking to him. Before long there was a wall between the workers and the managers that neither took the time to tear down.

I caught myself smiling that evening as I drove out of the plant. I was exhausted from working to keep the group calm long enough to get everything in line for the next day, but I was excited too. It's not often that a consultant gets to break away from the managers of a company to work directly with the people who add value to the product. The experts of the process have always been and will always be the operators, and no one can solve a problem faster than the group that does the work, when they are motivated.

We started the next day even earlier, at 6 am. The team was dressed for work in jeans and tee-shirts and they gave me a pretty hard time when I arrived wearing much the same outfit. They really laughed when they figured out I was wearing steel toed shoes, but I was trying to set a good example. Besides, I didn't have a single toe I was willing to do without.

The day was long. We moved out more than two large dumpsters full of trash, broken tools, broken containers, obsolete material, and basic junk from the work area. Then we cleaned everything with degreaser. The team still wasn't satisfied. They wanted a fresh coat of paint on everything. The clock said there was time, so we got started. Just about the time we were putting the stuff in the assigned locations, the subassembly team strolled back across the aisle.

They wanted to talk to us again about moving their process closer to the main line. They had apparently continued their discussion after we talked the last time and had come up with some pretty good ideas. We took some measurements for their fixturing and outlined placement for the WIP on the main line. Everything looked like it would fit with some minor maintenance and re-working the electricity and air, and we got the job done.

One of the discoveries in moving the subassembly process was that we could run the main line for over a week after the move without the subassembly processes running. The main line would exhaust the overproduction of work in process inventory and reduce the storage space required. This would free up the subassembly operators to help out on the main line while the operators learned the new flow, which should be able to speed up the process by more than 25%.

We attached the hand tools used by the operators to their workbench with retractable key chains to keep the tools at work height and readily available at all times. The operators said that this low cost fix would probably save them about 20% of their time, because they wouldn't have to look for tools throughout the shift.

At the end of the 2½ day session the team decided to

present the outcome of the workshop to the management staff and asked me to invite them to the presentation. We had the foresight to take some before and after pictures, so the impact was pretty impressive.

Leaning Into Six Sigma

Chapter Four

The Results of Good Housekeeping

The team was ready on the morning of the presentation. They had chosen to type up a list of their accomplishments and make copies for each of the managers in attendance at the presentation. They also decided to position themselves around the meeting room in a way that forced management to intermingle with operations employees to help foster open communication.

I took just a minute to introduce the group to the managers when the meeting kicked off, and the team members took over from there. As the most vocal of the group, Michelle was "volunteered" to speak for everyone. She was nervous, but her excitement provided her with the strength to get through the presentation. Michelle started in a surprisingly challenging manner, when she blatantly asked the managers, including Sid, "What the hell took you so long?"

She next proceeded to discuss what the team thought of the training and what they had learned. From there she

29

showed the before and after pictures, and wrapped up by reviewing the list of accomplishments, with the rest of the team chiming in where they were needed.

The managers asked several questions, and Michelle eventually told them that it would probably be easier to go out and physically review the changes. The difference was like night and day. Everything was clean and well organized, and the excess inventory was identified as waste.

After the team provided plant management with a tour of the process, we retreated back into the meeting room for a wrap-up discussion. Sid was first to speak. He stood up and looked at the team for what seemed like hours but what was probably only seconds. He was shaking his head the whole time as he stared, then finally spoke.

"I'm pleasantly surprised."

Sid looked directly at George when he made his next comment. "There were a lot of us in this company who did not believe you guys could do this. None of us believed you could accomplish as much as you have." Next Sid looked at me. "I have a new respect for my employees, and I'm embarrassed that it took an outside influence to bring this to light".

Sid went on to talk to his employees in an open and honest dialogue that included answering some basic questions about the state of the business. The operators were eager to provide more improvement suggestions and the entire room agreed at the end of the meeting to continue to apply the lessons learned the past week to the rest of the processes in the facility. Now this was what being "that guy" was all about!

Sid asked me to stay and talk with him after the wrap-up

meeting, and invited George to join us. We ended the discussion with the agreement that I would return the following week and we would take it one week at a time for the next month or so. Sid and George were starting to believe that we could seriously reduce costs without large capital investments. As I was leaving the office, Sid asked me to bring in the books on Six Sigma and Lean I had previously mentioned to him, so he could begin to better understand the concepts.

Back in the car, I was glad to be going home because I was completely exhausted from my week with Sid's employees, but I was also glad to be coming back the next week, because now they were my friends. Michelle had even invited me to join her family for a fish fry on my next visit to the plant. I hoped she would be ready by the next week when I came back, because home cooked fish really sounded good after a week of fast food and hotel cuisine.

Leaning Into Six Sigma

Chapter Five

Epiphany Déjà vu

Back in the plant, Sid asked me to look things over and decide where I would like to conduct the next workshop. I set up camp in the office where Celia sent me and headed out to the plant in order to find the next opportunity.

As I was finishing up for the day, I received a phone call from Sid's administrative assistant. Celia informed me that Sid wanted to see me in his office at 6 A.M. the next morning. He had a staff meeting at 10 A.M. and needed to be briefed on Six Sigma. He had done some research from the books I recommended and was not quite clear on the subject. "Not clear" I had learned (from past experience) meant confused. It was all I could do to keep from asking "What, again?"

I arrived the next morning promptly at 6 A.M. and found Sid pouring through a stack of books, all with Six Sigma strategically placed in the title. Scattered across the desk was a variety of periodicals and Internet printouts with the same title proclivities. So much for my *Lean Champion* and

33

Leaning Into Six Sigma

Understanding Workplace Organization. Sid looked like he was suffering from information overload. He hadn't even noticed I had walked into the room, so I said "good morning" and handed him a cup of coffee.

Sid looked up, took the cup of coffee and leaned back in his chair. "You're a consultant. What do you know about this Six Sigma stuff?"

I immediately wondered why he assumed that there was a link between being a consultant and understanding Six Sigma. Luckily I did understand. Unfortunately it would reinforce his convoluted thought process.

I responded "In my previous job I went through the Six Sigma training. I am a certified Black Belt and Master Black Belt."

"So you understand everything about Six Sigma?" Sid asked.

"I don't think I really understand everything about Six Sigma, but I will try to help you. Celia said you were conf….. unclear about some things. What can I help you with?" I asked.

Sid began "I have read all this stuff, and it is really difficult to determine what Six Sigma is. Some of these tell me it is a philosophy. Some a quality program. All are full of statistics that are talking about things I don't really understand. It seems they all talk about saving money with some kind of connection to quality. That seems to be an oxymoron in my experience."

"There are a variety of opinions on what Six Sigma is" I told him. "It actually began in 1964 when Juran wrote his book *Managerial Breakthrough.* The book distinguishes between control - an absence of change; and breakthrough -

change. That is really an abridged version of the book, but we don't have a lot of time. Motorola initiated the program around 1986 and really perfected some techniques around it. A few companies, such as Texas Instruments and ABB picked it up. It really came to prominence with the deployments at Allied Signal and General Electric in the mid-90's."

"Thanks for the history lesson, but I still don't know what it is," Sid said.

"It seems to be different things to different companies," I explained. "There are basic elements which are common among all the companies which have deployed Six Sigma. The program centers around using a problem solving methodology called M-A-I-C. That stands for Measure, Analyze, Improve and Control. They are the four steps used in the Six Sigma problem solving methodology. The methodology is used on projects which are chronic problems selected for Black Belts to work on."

"What is a Black Belt and where did the project come from?" Sid interrupted.

"Black Belts are people who have gone through a training process and completed projects to gain certification in the Six Sigma problem solving methodology. These projects should be chronic problems that are strategically aligned with the company's business objectives. They are selected by Champions." I said

"So what is a Champion and where did they come from?" Sid asked.

"The Champions are typically selected by the Leadership Team. They are people with credibility, influence, and usually some level of formal power inside the organization. In the Champion role they are the interface between the strategic plans of the organization and the operational level. Are you clear on everything so far?" I asked.

Sid thought a moment and asked, "It sounds like a pretty easy job just picking things for other people to work on. Do they do anything else?"

"The Champion role is not a full time position" I replied. "An equally important role is to remove barriers for the Black Belt as they work on their projects. The job normally takes about 20 to 30 percent of their time."

"So these Champions are going to spend about eight to twelve hours a week supporting a Black Belt?" Sid inquired.

"That would assume they work a 40 hour week now." I replied. "Actually how much time they have to spend dealing with barriers is up to you."

"How's that?" Sid asked.

"The initiatives all deal with change to the organization. Remember Juran's distinction between control and breakthrough. I am sure in your reading you have seen Six Sigma referred to as a Breakthrough Strategy. Accepting that definition means you are embarking on a change program."

"Like I said….. What's that got to do with me?" Sid interjected.

"Well, we said that some of the most recognized programs were at Motorola under Robert Galvin, Allied Signal under Larry Bossidy, and GE under Jack Welch. None of these gentlemen were spectators during the program. They sent very clear messages which were visible at all levels of the organization, that they stood solidly

Leaning Into Six Sigma

behind these programs and they expected every level of the organization to respond. Leadership in abstencia doesn't work when you expect serious change. Clearly defining and communicating the company's expectation only belongs to the highest level of leadership in the company, and that is you."

"So you mean you want me to tell everyone in the company that this is my program?" Sid asked.

"Exactly and repeatedly. It is the only way it stands a chance of working." I replied.

"Okay, I got it. Isn't this the same stuff I read about in that book *The Fifth Discipline*? What was it they called it... intrinsic and extrinsic messages?" Sid wondered out loud.

"Exactly. It is more than just what you say, it is also what you do. I believe there have been several books, periodical articles, etc., which have reiterated the benefits of communication. If you will remember the idea of MBWA, *Management By Walking Around*, from Tom Peters. Same kind of thing. Visible leadership isn't new, but it is an idea still waiting for its time."

"All right, I'll check my schedule and see how much extra time I have. You said you were a Master Black Belt. So what is that?" Sid asked.

"Some Black Belts are chosen to receive additional training after they are certified, to become Master Black Belts." I replied.

"What do they do?" Sid asked.

"The Master Black Belts mentor the Black Belts and train new Black Belts." I replied.

"What do all these Six Sigma consultants do then?" Sid asked.

Leaning Into Six Sigma

"The first few waves of Black Belts in an organization are trained and certified by the consultants. They help choose the Master Black Belts and certify them as well. When there is a competent core of Master Black Belts trained, there really isn't any more need for consultants. Their job is to get the company to the point where they have their own stand-alone program. The Master Black Belts should be the exit ticket for the consultants." I replied.

"Alright, I think I am starting to get it. We have Champions, Master Black Belts, and Black Belts who work on projects. The projects address chronic problems, and projects should be strategically aligned with the objectives of the company. That about it so far?" Sid asked.

"Visible leadership?" I asked

"Oh, yeah and visible leadership. That was my job, right?" Sid asked.

"I believe that would be you, yes. Shall we continue?" I asked.

"Sure. Remember I have a staff meeting at ten." Sid said.

During the next hour I explained to Sid that regardless of the different window dressings that various consulting companies had hung on Six Sigma, it revolved around a basic problem solving equation $Y = f(x)$ or $Y = f\ x_1 + x_2 + x_3$ ... This equation defined the relationship between a dependent variable, Y, and independent variables, the x's. The problem solving equation served as a guide for the Six Sigma Methodology of MAIC.

During the *Measure Phase* the project focus, the problem, was the Y. Various tools such as process mapping, basic statistics, capability studies, I/O matrix, and measurement system analysis were used to define and quantify the project. Besides the statistical tools we also would write a problem statement, project objective, and form a team. The financial impact of the problem and the potential solution to the problem are assessed. Members of the company's financial community must assist and concur with the assessment as well.

After the Measurement Phase was complete we moved on to the *Analyze Phase*. Following the *Problem Solving Equation*, during this phase we would begin to identify the various x's which were causing the Y to behave in an unacceptable manner. As we identify the various x's, hypothesis testing is used to either verify or disprove the various theories and assumptions the team had developed around the causal systems affecting the Y.

Once the Analysis Phase was completed we moved to the *Improve Phase*. It is during this phase that *Regression Analyze* and *Design of Experiments* is used to identify the relationships between the x's. The x's are the independent variables associated with the Y, but that does not mean they are independent of each other. Variables such as temperature and pressure affect each other and the interaction of the two also affect the Y. We can never completely understand the effect of an interaction without the use of Design of Experiments. It is the complete understanding of the x's that allows us to arrive at an optimized solution to the problem at the end of the Improve Phase.

Now that we have a solution to the problem, we move to the *Control Phase* to institutionalize the solution. During this phase tools such as mistake proofing, quality systems, and control charts are leveraged to make sure that the problem is eliminated for good.

Leaning Into Six Sigma

Sid thanked me for my time and left for his meeting. Feeling that he had become clear on the basics of Six Sigma, I returned to the factory to continue where I had left off the day before. I had been around management long enough that I should have realized it would not be quite that simple.

Although it was a short walk back to the factory, I had only been there a short time when Celia called. My presence was requested immediately in the executive conference room. I hung up and started back towards the conference room. Intuitively I should have known that there is a strong positive correlation between clarity of understanding and time. I had not spent enough time to significantly impact the dependent variable, clarity. I had not realized the impact the Six Sigma training had had on me until I realized I was even analyzing communication as dependent and independent variables. Maybe it wasn't a problem after all, since understanding the concept facilitated a total understanding. It was only through the understanding that I could make improvements. What was that saying "You have to translate the practical problem into a numerical problem before you can analyze it. You only gain knowledge through the analysis."

I was starting to understand understanding. This was getting way too deep. Wrong frame of mind for a management meeting. It was time to focus on emotion, tribal knowledge, and the politically correct.

When I entered the conference room the tension was so thick you could have cut it with a knife. How could a discussion of a data driven, problem solving program create this much emotion? It wasn't as if it was an unproven entity. Six Sigma had been implemented all over the world. I assumed that the addition, subtraction, multiplication and division that drove the statistics would work the same here as it did in the rest of the world. Maybe the issue was the data driven decision making. The gurus always feel threatened. Kind of a territorial thing, I think. Time to enter the lion's den.

Sid motioned to a chair to his left, which probably did not give the impression of perceived power it could have if I would have been on the right, but it was at his end of the table. I guess it would have to do.

Sid introduced me to his staff and then spoke directly to me. "We discussed the basics of a Six Sigma program but it seems there are a few more issues. We would like to get your expert opinion on them."

"I will try to answer any questions you have." I told him, thinking to myself that it was nice to have the president characterize my opinions as expert, even though I wasn't sure what data he had used to determine that.

Sid began "The idea of Six Sigma was initiated by our CFO, Bill Payer. Bill has read the reports about the large financial returns that many companies are reporting from using the *Breakthrough Strategy*. Bill feels if it yields this level of return on investment, then we should get some of this breakthrough for our manufacturing. Our Vice President of Manufacturing is taking exception to the insinuation that we are wasting that much money in our factories. They have already been engaged in many improvement initiatives such as TQM. He doesn't believe there is much opportunity in our factories. What do you think?"

"First we need to make it clear that the Six Sigma has never been a manufacturing program," I explained. "Even when it was introduced at Motorola, the objective was to be Six Sigma in everything we do, which included non-manufacturing operations. GE Capital, as well as many other financial institutions, call centers, and public utilities have all had successful deployments. The financial returns are well documented. Most legitimate Six Sigma providers require that the financial community sign off on any claims about savings. Many of the larger companies are reporting these savings in their Annual Reports, which are signed off on by major accounting firms. I probably wouldn't know about it if it happened, but I haven't seen anyone standing up in shareholders meetings to tell some of the most powerful CEO's in the country that their savings numbers are inflated."

I looked around the room to see if they were following me, then continued, "As far as there not being any opportunities left because we have already done TQM. You have to understand that there is a continuum of tools and techniques. When you reach a certain level, you have to find a way to move to the next level. It isn't an issue of who is better, it is simply choosing the correct tool for the job. Not every problem is a Six Sigma project, so if you can fix it with TQM, then that is what you use.

"If you want to get some of this breakthrough it takes work. It isn't for sale. Dr. Deming told the story about the man who offered to pay him for the formula for good quality. He would pay anything. Dr. Deming said there isn't such a thing as instant pudding. We couldn't buy it then and it still can't be bought today. Eliminating defects, waste and effecting change is a function of hard work. Period."

Sid said "Thank you for the input. We do have another

issue. Our Vice President of Quality feels that Six Sigma isn't anything new, it is just the same collection of tools that have always been around. We have trained a lot of people on how to use these tools already. Besides, these Six Sigma consultants charge a lot of money. You have been through the training, what do you think?"

"The point of Six Sigma is not, and never was, to introduce new tools. We really don't need any new tools at this point, since we rarely use the more sophisticated ones that we have. The Six Sigma Methodology focuses on being able to link the tools together into a logical flow. Data is moved from one tool to another so that there is a synergy between the tools. It is that synergy that increases the probability of problem resolution," I told him.

I could see several nods of comprehension, so I moved on, tackling the financial issue. "As far as what the consultants are paid, it is a business decision. It is a value proposition. Most credible Six Sigma providers have track records of verifiable results. It is not just a training program for the sake of training. A Black Belt candidate who doesn't produce results doesn't get certified. If you are really concerned with the cost, offer them a revenue sharing proposition. Most have been in the business long enough that they will sign up for this faster than you will. They believe in their product."

Sid thanked me for the information and asked if there were any other questions. Nobody had any further questions. Sid told them I was already working in the factory, and if they had any other questions that they could find me through Celia. I was sure this would not be the end.

Leaning Into Six Sigma

Chapter Six

The Crow's Nest

I started back to the factory feeling somewhat better about Sid's understanding of what Six Sigma and Lean are, and their applicability to S.G., Inc. However, I still had some antacids left and I was pretty sure they were going to come in handy before we were done.

I had hardly cleared the entry door to the factory when George walked in. "Sam, do you have a few minutes?" "Sure" I said, "what can I help you with?" George was looking unusually serious so I figured whatever it was, it deserved my undivided attention. "Sam, before we go any further there are a couple of things I need to get off my chest. First, I have to tell you when Sid told me he was going to bring you in to get a second opinion on which machine we should buy, I was *not* a happy camper. I have pretty much run this entire operation for the past fifteen years and if there was anything I was sure of, it was that I didn't need any

45

outsider to tell me how to do my job. And second, I have to admit that this morning I sat in the crow's nest and watched Michelle's group for a couple of hours. I've haven't seen that esprit de corps around here in ten years. It was like we transplanted a whole new team of employees in that area. I also timed the process, and believe it or not, they have reduced the cycle time by over 25% in less than a week! It reminded me of the old days when we all worked as a team, when we all took pride in our product, our customers, and our company. It was fun then. If we could get that attitude throughout the plant, we would be a world class organization. Anyway, enough running off at the mouth for me, so here is what I came to ask you. Remember the first day you came to the plant and I gave you a tour?"

"Of course I do, George," I told him.

"If you have time, I would like for *you* to give *me* a tour of the plant and let's talk about what you see. I guess what I'm getting at, is if I were sitting in a crow's nest looking down at the entire plant, what would I look for? How do we make this happen?"

"I would be delighted. Let's walk over to receiving, we'll start there," I suggested. "While we're walking, George, let me ask you a question. You said if you could get that attitude throughout the plant, S.G., Inc. could be a world class organization, right?"

"Yes, I think we could."

"The question then is, if all the manufacturing processes in your plant were Six Sigma would you be a world class plant?"

"Sure," George said, "that would mean we would only have about three defects per million opportunities, based on what you told us in the meeting on Monday. Isn't that about as good as it gets?"

"I see," I told him. "We'll talk about this more later, but, food for thought, if you send your perfect product to your customer two weeks late, is that a world class organization?"

"Yeah, I see what you mean," he agreed. "But if the processes are Six Sigma, why would the product ever be late getting to the customer?"

"Let's see if we can answer that question during the tour."

We were walking past the fleet of tractor trailers I noticed my first day here to finally get to a raw material warehouse. George told me they had completed this 10,000 square foot building about a year ago. According to George, they had simply run out of storage space. The building looked great except for a huge dent in the top of the tractor trailer entry door.

"What happened here?" as if I didn't know.

George grinned sheepishly and mocking the tone of an instructor said, "We didn't design the door tall enough for the big semis. Maybe the planning stage of this project needed a little more work."

We both had a good laugh and walked inside.

The warehouse was ostensibly neat and orderly. Ostensibly being the key word here. With the exception of the tractor trailer entry aisle, there were five rows of fifteen foot high shelving running the length of the building, housing all the small parts and raw stock in cardboard boxes with the contents written on the box. On the back wall were stacks of 4 foot by 8 foot by 6 inch plate stacked 20 high with 4 inch square wooden blocks between them so they could be handled by forklift. All the plate stock coding (part number, PO number, cert number, etc.) was written on the face of the plate with a black marker. Between the front wall and the shelving were wooden pallets on which the heavier parts and pre-sawed raw stock was kept.

"If Sid called you and said, 'George, we've got a hot one. We need ten of these parts by tomorrow,' and to make those parts you need that bottom piece of plate, how long would it take you to get that plate to the saw?"

George pondered for a moment then started calculating under his breath, "Let's see, there are 19 pieces of plate on top of it, we have to get the fork over here, each piece would take about five minutes to move....oh, about two hours or so."

"George, what do you see here? Remember the conversations we have had on 5S and waste reduction? Think about it as though you were in a "firefighting" mode, and you needed something quickly from this warehouse, what would cause you frustration?"

"That's easy," he said, "two things, in fact. First, the stuff on the shelves we can never find, and second, the plate stock and the parts on the pallets. It sometimes takes hours to dig it out of there."

"Good observations."

" Wait a minute, Sam. You're supposed to be giving me the tour. Give me an overview of what *you* think could be done to make the warehouse more efficient."

"Without getting too detailed, here are a couple of things you might consider:

- You have told me you have five times the inventory

you need in here. Make arrangements with your venders to take select inventory (based on need, PO's, backlog, etc.) back for credit.
- Get with Purchasing, start working the rest down to a realistic level
- Evaluate your vendors, partner with select ones for better service and quality assurance
- Label the shelving (row, bin, etc.)
- All pallets on labeled shelves
- Plastic part boxes for small parts
- Vertical storage for the plate stock using the hoist for quick retrieval
- Returnable dunnage

"And," George chimed in, "with a good labeling system, we can computerize all the parts and locations. We could find anything in here quicker'n a hiccup."

"George, I think you're beginning to get the hang of it. One other thing I want to mention before we leave the warehouse. Do you see the downstream impact of two hours wasted in the warehouse on the total cycle time of a delivered product?"

"Absolutely, we could add several hours to the delivery of that ten piece order you were talking about just in warehouse inefficiencies alone. But the real kicker is that the same potential for waste is at every step throughout the entire manufacturing process from the saw, to the lathe, to well... everything."

"You're absolutely right George, but not just manufacturing. Six Sigma, 5S, workplace organization and waste elimination are just as applicable in administrative areas as they are in manufacturing."

"By the way, Sam, I'm also beginning to see how it's possible for our manufacturing processes to be at Six Sigma and not be anywhere near world class. What do you say we go over to the plant and continue? This is great stuff."

As we walked the hundred yards or so back to the plant, George was verbally mapping out a plan to have a team address workplace organization issues in the warehouse area. I suggested that he might ask a person from Purchasing to join the team so they could become more aware of each other's unique situations and/or problems. He agreed that was a good idea.

"We've got to get these people trained in Six Sigma/Lean logic so we can get started ASAP. The more people we can get working on projects and improving their respective work areas and processes, the quicker we develop the overall cultural transformation we need, the quicker we become more competitive, and the quicker we get our deliveries back on schedule. But even more importantly, the quicker we get our corporate pride back."

We arrived back at the plant, walked in the back door, and the first thing George had to say was, "Ah yes," pointing to a CNC machine. "Sam, #14 here is one of our problem children. This machine must have a ghost living in it. This thing will run like a Swiss watch for a while and "bam!" for no apparent reason, it spits out bad parts. Our people, the manufacturer's reps., and anyone else who might have a suggestion has taken a shot at fixing this one. "Joe," said George, "get me a rag. I want to wipe off the gauges and see what's she's running like this week."

"Joe," I asked, "do the PM (preventive maintenance),

scrap sheets or repair records give you any indication of what's causing the problems?"

"I'm the only one who runs this machine," Joe told me. "In fact, I'm the only person who has run this machine for the past eight years. I know her like the back of my hand. I do all the maintenance, so there's no reason to keep up with that stuff. In fact, I know this machine so well I can tell when the fluids need changing by smell alone."

I couldn't believe what I was hearing! Here is a bottleneck in the production process, and it's a machine so filthy you can't tell what color it is. There were jigs, tools, old die parts, scrapped parts, oily rags, old gloves, magazines, mounds of chips, and even an old chair for the operator to do absolutely nothing more comfortably. And as one might expect, there was a small mountain of incoming material on one side of machine #14 and the next process was setting idle waiting for parts.

George walked toward me with that perplexed look again. "Sam, something just dawned on me. We have just proven that we can eliminate waste in the warehouse through 5S and workplace organization. Granted, the warehouse will be more efficient, but if I get the material over here and it just sits waiting for the next process, have I really gained anything?

"Good observation, George. Let's go to your office and talk about that crow's nest overview."

When we got to George's office we both got a cup of coffee. I noticed that George had copies of some of the periodicals and Internet printouts that I had seen on Sid's desk. Good. I launched right into an answer.

"The reason SG, Inc. is still in business is that you are

providing a product somebody wants and they are willing to pay you to make it for them. Right? Over the past couple of decades there have been significant changes, such as technological innovations, information access, new international players, etc., that make it more and more difficult to remain profitable and stay in business. It wasn't that long ago the formula for determining the price we were going to charge for our product was simple; $P=C+M$. We determined how much it cost to make the product, added the margin we required, and that was the price."

George nodded his agreement, so I continued, "Today, largely as a result of communication intelligence, a customer can do business in another country almost as easily as they used to in an adjoining city. The result is that we have smarter, better informed customers today, with options they never had before. To remain competitive in the market we have had to change our formula. Today's customer has a large influence on the price, and we therefore, must salvage an acceptable margin by eliminating costs through smarter, more efficient operations.

"That's where Six Sigma and Lean come in. Lean addresses continuous improvement, 5S, waste identification and elimination, workplace organization, VA and NVA, vendor relationships, SMED, TPM, visual factories, error proofing, process standardization, culture changes, physical arrangement of the facility, etc....that promote and insure an efficient, synchronous flow of products and information throughout the organization.

"While Lean eliminates 'noise' and establishes a standard, Six Sigma and it's tools are used to resolve any negative deviations from that standard. So with the complement of Six Sigma and Lean, the proverbial bar is perpetually raised."

"So,"said George, "what you're saying is, on machine #14 for example, clean up that mess down there, *Lean* that process, get rid of the "noise" as you called it, then we can use the Six Sigma tools to deal with variation, and finally get to the root cause of our quality problem."

"There's a little more to it than that, but yes," I agreed. "Remember the formula $Y=f(x)_1 + (x)_2 + (x)_3 \ldots$ If you want the Y to perform in a specific acceptable range, you must identify and control the x variables."

The phone rang and George answered. It was Sid. After a short conversation and a few tidbits of profanity, George hung up. "Sorry Sam, we're going to have to put all this on hold until after the first of the month. Here it is the 25th and it doesn't look like we are going to make our numbers this month. Sid's on the warpath and wants to do some rescheduling. He wants me to shut down Michelle's line this afternoon, retool it and pull some PO's from next month so we can book them. You know how it is. Let's see, Monday is the 2nd, call me then and we will get started again. Things are usually pretty quiet the first couple of weeks of the month."

Leaning Into Six Sigma

Chapter Seven

Some Things Never Change

As I walked away from my conversation and tour through the plant with George, I couldn't help shaking my head. All the talk and all the eye opening conversations still hadn't changed his approach to managing his business. It was still just project work. It was still firefighting to get the numbers.

I walked by Michelle's operation as I headed toward the front office. She yelled at me from across the aisle and asked me to come over and talk. As I approached her station she looked up and asked "Who let the air out of your tires?" I looked up and smiled because it was hard not to smile when Michelle talked to you. She was that kind of person. I started to explain what had just occurred with George, but when I looked up and saw her expression I knew I should stop talking and listen for a few minutes.

"Don't give up on us, you can't! Just keep working with George, he'll get it eventually. We all think that George is a smart guy and he wants to make things better, you just have to give him some time to understand."

I didn't say much in reply, although I probably should have. I just smiled and nodded at her as I walked away. Of course she was right.

I kept thinking through the problem at hand and just as I walked into the office doors I made a decision. I didn't so much as walk over to Celia's office as I ran, and I almost fell over when I realized that she was happy to see me. She wasn't just smiling, she was genuinely happy. Celia actually stopped what she was doing and asked me how she could help. In all the weeks I had been working with SG, she had never even pretended to want to help me with anything. Maybe things weren't so bad after all.

"Celia, ah.. I mean Ms. Gordon, would you mind scheduling the large conference room for George and me tomorrow?"

Once again she caught me off guard with her response, "Oh please Sam, call me Celia. "With all the wonderful things I've been hearing about the work you are doing around here, I'm happy to help you out!"

After I stammered out the time I would like to have the conference room reserved, I walked back to my makeshift work space and started making plans.

Later that day I made sure I just happened to be leaving the facility as George was walking out the door. I walked over to him and asked for a minute or two of his time. George said he was on his way to grab a sandwich and a beer and invited me to join him. I responded in the affirmative "Beats the heck out of my hotel room service." He nodded and we walked out to our respective cars. George shouted over his shoulder, "Just follow me" as he got in and started the engine.

I followed George off the plant property and out into the country. When the blacktop turned into a lightly graveled dirt road, I wasn't quite sure I was going to enjoy this sandwich and beer. We turned into what appeared to be a dirt parking lot and shut off our engines. While I was mildly amused at the roundabout way we had to go to get to the location, I had to admit that the setting was beautiful. The bar was tucked under a stand of trees that bordered a small but quickly moving river.

"OK, I'm trusting you on this one George," I laughed as we walked toward the open-air bar.

He grinned as usual and said, "You won't be sorry."

We walked in and sat on two of the mismatched chairs and George ordered Coronas and Cuban sandwiches for both of us. After he had shouted our order, he turned back to me and said "Remember, you trust me."

We started shelling peanuts and dropping the shells on the dirt floor while the bar owner made the sandwiches behind the bar.

"I've been thinking about our conversation this morning George," I started the conversation head-on. "Something has been eating at me all day. Did you notice that even after we reviewed all the process issues in the facility, your last input to the discussion was that you had to fight fires again at the end of this month?"

I stopped short of asking what was wrong with him. Michelle was right, this guy was not dumb. The expression on his face told me he had already been thinking of this very issue and was ready to talk about how to break the vicious, not-so-smooth circle of activities he was using to manage the business.

As George popped the last peanut into his mouth, the conversation began in earnest. We were talking so much that we hardly noticed when the bar owner brought the Cubans and beers, but all conversation halted as I took my first bite of the sandwich.

"Oh… my… *gosh…!* This has got to be the best Cuban sandwich I have ever tasted! How did you ever find this place?"

George explained through mouthfuls that the bar owner, Gloria, had actually been his fifth grade teacher, and this bar was her retirement plan. He spent as much time in the place as possible to help supplement her income, and he also brought in as many people as were willing to eat in her fine establishment. "Well, you've got me hooked," I said between mouthfuls, "She can count on my business as least once a week as long as I'm working with SG".

George and I laughed as he yelled the good news across the bar to Gloria. She said she wasn't surprised and brought us another Corona without asking. This was a woman who knew how to satisfy her customers, not to mention how to get those extra sales dollars. Nothing wrong with being a good business person.

As we finished our sandwiches, George and I also finished putting together a plan of attack for breaking his firefighting mode and tackling the organizational issues directly at the root.

We parted ways after another beer or two with the decision that we would meet in the large conference room at the plant first thing tomorrow morning. I didn't tell George that I had already reserved the room. He might not have realized that in reserving it, I was just proving my belief that he would do the smart thing and decide to get down to working toward real solutions to his problems.

Leaning Into Six Sigma

Chapter Eight

Eliminating the Waste

George was surprised when he walked into the conference room at the beginning of the shift. I was already making notes on the white board, and Michelle's entire work team was sitting around the large conference table. I had written in large bold letters at the top of the board:

BALANCING WORK FLOW

As George took his seat, the chatter in the room died down and we began the meeting. I started off by explaining that by taking the crows nest view it was evident that Michelle's process was still the bottleneck. We had to find a way to eliminate the capacity issue and free up some extra time so that they could run in sync with the rest of the plant.

I started to facilitate a brainstorming session when Michelle stood up and suggested that we move to the factory floor. Everyone thought that was an excellent idea so we picked up our flip chart and walked out to the process. The night shift had agreed to stay over an hour to continue the

61

process while we conducted the meeting and they were hard at work when we walked up to the line.

The work the team had completed made it very easy to see the flow of the process. Material and quality issues were readily apparent just by looking, and the brainstorming list grew faster than I could write down their ideas.

"Whoa! I can't keep up with you guys, slow down. Or better yet, who wants to take over as scribe for this session?" George didn't really volunteer, he just took the pen from me and started writing. Relieved from my hand cramp, I had an opportunity to watch the process for a while. I turned to George and said, "Add rework to the list."

George started to write down rework, but Michelle stepped up and stopped him. In fact, the entire team turned around and looked at me like I was crazy. Bob, one of the newer employees on the line, spoke up.

"What are you talking about? We don't have any rework on this line. Our first time yield on this process is over 98%."

I held my hands up to stop Bob from going on.

"Wait, Wait, Wait! I'm not trying to insinuate that you guys are doing a poor job. I just want to make sure we capture all the opportunities available to us."

Michelle spoke up next. "Well what are you talking about then, Sam? We don't see any defects on the line. The scrap bins are empty and there is nothing piling up for quality inspection."

I couldn't argue. The team had done a great job of setting up a visual workplace. It was simple to see where the problems were, and from a casual observation, no there didn't appear to be any problems. But, when I took a closer look, something didn't seem quite right.

Leaning Into Six Sigma

"Well, let's talk about the tools you are using to complete the tasks at this process. George, flip the page on the chart and let's list all the tools we are using for each station," I suggested.

George began writing as we dictated a complete list of all of the tools being used in the process:

1. Impact Wrenches
2. Rubber Mallet
3. Square
4. Drill for Reaming
5. Tap
6. Hoist

As we finished the list the class turned back to me.

Bob asked again, "Okay Sam, where is the rework?"

I started to explain when I heard one of the other operators gasp. "It's the reamer," she said, "we are using the reamer on every unit!"

Michelle shook her head "It can't be the reamer, we can't build parts without it. The reamer is not rework, it's part of the job."

I prompted Michelle for more information about the process, and in particular what exactly caused them to ream every unit of production. As I spoke I started timing the process of reaming the holes in the unit. Michelle spent the next several minutes explaining to me the process of reaming. "Sam, I've been working on this line for more than 20 years and we have always reamed these holes. You can't expect to join three pieces of metal together in multiple locations without reaming the holes so that bolts can fit through them." She smiled kindly and went on to explain, "If we don't ream the holes, the unit won't be square, and the components down the line won't fit properly. So you see Sam, reaming isn't rework, it's just part of the process. Nice try though".

"Well Michelle," I explained, "while you were talking just now I timed three cycles of production and the reaming adds over five minutes to the total cycle time for your process." I didn't want to push too hard, but I needed to make sure that she understood where I was trying to lead her. "What if the holes lined up perfectly when the parts were stamped? Would you still have to ream the holes?"

While Michelle thought about my question, Bob spoke up, "Of course you wouldn't have to ream anything. But if you think you could ever stamp those holes perfectly, you're nuts!" At the end of Bob's statement the crowd paused a second and then let out a loud laugh.

I knew it was important that I continue my discussion while they were still laughing. "Okay, okay, but *if* we could stamp the parts perfectly, that would eliminate the reaming process, right?"They all continued to snicker, but Michelle shook her head yes.

I pressed on, "So if we could eliminate the reaming process, would our cycle time balance out better with the main line?"

George had been pretty quiet up to this point but he finally spoke up. "If we could drop the reaming process, we would be able to eliminate all the overtime from this process, and still work slightly faster than the main line. But I have to agree with the team on this one, Sam. I don't think it can be done." George went on to explain that they had looked at the stamping process a couple of times. The equipment was in good shape and the engineering group couldn't find any problems with the program.

We didn't notice while we were talking but Sid had walked up behind us and was listening to the conversation George and I were having. After George finished explaining why the reaming process couldn't be eliminated, I asked him to have the engineer and the stamp press operator paged to the stamping building so we could have a look at the process.

George looked skeptical but he had the two men paged and asked them to meet me in the stamping building. Michelle said I was crazy and proceeded to round up her team so they could get back on their process. As I walked over to the stamping building, I wondered if I had lost my mind. This was going to be a long day. Man I love this job.

At 11 P.M. that evening, I walked out of the plant and shook the hands of the two men who had stayed with me to look at the process for more than fourteen hours. They were good men and they had done a good job. I was glad that we had taken the time to look at the process. I was just about to open the door on my car when I heard someone call my name from across the parking lot.

"Sam, hey Sam, wait up!" I turned to see George and Sid running toward me. "We couldn't leave while you were working out there all night, but we didn't want to interrupt." George said.

Sid went on "I stopped by a couple of times to see how things were going but you three were huddled so tightly that I figured I'd just let you go at it. How did it go Sam, did you figure out what was going on that causes the holes to be misaligned?"

I was surprised to see the two of them standing there this late in the evening, but I was happy that they were interested enough to wait to see what we had found out. My answer was not what they wanted to hear. "No, I didn't figure it out. We looked at everything; the program, the specification, the equipment."

I continued by explaining that everything had been within the tolerance limits defined by the design engineers and that we couldn't find a reason for the misalignment.

Brian, the engineer, looked at the program for most of the night, but couldn't find any fault in the logic. Jason, the stamping operator, showed me the dies and the set up tools he used, and we couldn't find anything wrong there either. Finally around 9 P.M. we all sat down and had coffee. I asked Jason to talk to me about what had been done on the process over the past twenty years. Jason explained that he had been running the process since it was started. He surprised me by reaching into his back pocket and pulling out a small notebook. Jason had kept process notes on everything that had been done since the very beginning.

I asked if I could take a quick look at his notes and found them to be particularly well laid out and very complete. I didn't see anything that would lead me to believe that the process had been disrupted in any way. I picked up my coffee was finishing off the last of it when Jason got a strange look on his face

"You know, there *was* one thing," he remembered. "It's probably nothing, but when we were setting up the process, we couldn't be sure which side of the die was supposed to be facing up. The process supervisor came out with the engineering team and measured the die and all the locator pins and they decided that the die was symmetric. The engineers said that since the die was equal on all sides it didn't really matter which side we put face up. We marked the die so we could be sure we always used it exactly the same way and we've been using it that way each time we set up the machine."

I looked at Jason and he read my mind. The coffee cups were in the trash can and we were running back to the process, with Brian following close behind. We didn't want to wait until the next day to check our theory, so we decided to set up the machine and run parts right then and there.

We stamped enough parts for one unit of production in the assembly process and had the parts moved to the main line for a trial run. Michelle's team was long gone from the morning shift but the third shift team was more than happy to help. We threaded in the unit we had just stamped, and as they laid the parts on the fixture, Jason, Bob, and I held our breath. One of the operators, a nice guy named Marty, came over with a reamer, but I stepped up just as he was moving into position.

"Can you try bolting it up without reaming?" I asked.

He looked at me and shrugged, "Sure, but I've been doing this for over five years, and I've never seen a frame go together without reaming. I don't see why it would start working now."

Marty was kind enough to humor me, and handed his co-workers the bolts for the frame. As they positioned them on the fixture, their mouths dropped open and all eyes shifted to me when the bolt slipped neatly into the holes.

Leaning Into Six Sigma

The first bombardment of questions was centered on the insistence that we must have drilled the holes out in the stamping department before we brought the parts over. I explained to the assembly team what we had discovered, and they replied that, just as they had always suspected, we were all a bunch of idiots.

I agreed, we must have been crazy to have allowed this to go on for twenty years, but never the less, the problem would be solved from here on out.

As I finished explaining our findings to Sid and George, I noticed a puzzled look on George's face. "Sam, I thought you said you didn't figure out what was wrong with the process." I explained to him that I didn't find the solution. Jason had remembered the problem, and when it had been generated. His notes and memory had allowed us to "fix" the problem.

Sometimes, listening to our operators can prevent waste in the processes. I finished opening my car door and looked at Sid, "You have a lot of great people in this company, Sid. Make sure you take advantage of their willingness to provide improvement ideas." I said goodnight and got in the car to drive away. It had indeed been a long day, but I wasn't crazy. Man, I love this job!

Chapter Nine

Full Circle: Lean to Six Sigma to Lean to Six Sigma

I received a phone call from George one morning a few weeks after we had corrected the stamping process. His voice sounded a little odd. He asked if I could stop by his office sometime that morning. George believed he had found a process where using Lean, Six Sigma, or a combination of the two wouldn't solve his problem. I wasn't sure if he was asking for help or wanting to gloat, since I had made a bet with him a few weeks before that he couldn't find a problem we couldn't solve using the tools. Either way, I told him I would stop by in a few minutes. I did not want him to think I was even the slightest bit afraid to deal with a problem.

When I arrived at George's office I was relieved to see I had totally misjudged his motives from the phone conversation. He was not gloating. He wanted help. He was more frustrated than I had seen him since my first days in the plant. George had seen enough of the various projects that he

69

had recognized the potential help he would be able to get from the two programs. He had even reached the level where he supported the two programs publicly.

George was getting faith. He had not hit the religious level yet; unfortunately he had found a situation where it seemed it would not work. His faith was shaken and I am sure he was concerned about the public stand he had taken. From my (purely selfish) standpoint I was not ready to lose George's support and commitment. It was critical that I find a way to prove to him once and for all that the tools, and more specifically I, would not let him down. I also wanted to make sure that after he had shown support to the program and the methodology, that I not allow him to find any reason to change his mind.

George explained that there was a subassembly process where compounds were mixed to form a rubberized product that was used later in many of the products produced by SG. Because this compound was formulated off the main line, it was considered a subassembly process. One of the key issues with the subassembly process was that it ran slower than the production line. Even though it was not part of the main line, it was the bottleneck in that all other processes were controlled by availability of material from our project process.

As George explained the situation it became apparent that the only reason it was not viewed as a problem for the organization was that running overtime each day made up the shortages. The overtime seemed to solve the capacity issue, however it did have its drawbacks. There had been times when the material that was queued up on the off shift had been defective. This created more than just a defect issue because when the production line out ran the mixer, there was no ability to catch up during the day. A day of production was lost when the line had to be shut down while the mixing process built a queue so the line could run continuously.

There had been another situation where there had been a problem on the production line. The problem had caused most of the material on the main production line to be scrapped. The mixing process had surfaced quickly as a bottleneck when the main line speed was increased in an effort to recover.

George continued to explain that although the problem with the mixer had been disguised with the queue, otherwise known as Work in Process (WIP). Realizing that this process was critical to the success of the facility, he had selected it early on for the initial Lean classes. The operators on the line had gone through the 5S and Standardized Work classes and reduced some of the queue, however it was still a bottleneck.

Next, they had targeted it for process optimization with the Six Sigma tools and still didn't get enough extra capacity to eliminate the queue. Finally, after all the recommendations from the Six Sigma program had been implemented, George had had the team do the 5S and Standardized Work again since the process had changed.

George had genuinely believed that all this work would get him enough extra capacity to eliminate the queue. But the mixing process was still too slow. He was at a loss as to where to go next.

After a short discussion I found out that the mixer they were using was an older unit. It was still capable, but due to normal use and wear it had lost some of its inherent capability. There was another mixer in the plant. The second mixer was newer, but when the team had attempted to mix the formulation on the newer mixer, they had been unsuccessful in producing a compound that met specification. They had run some long term capability studies and found it was running at just over a 0.33 Cpk or one standard deviation from the specification limit. George had not figured out a lot of the statistics, but he had figured out that One Sigma was less than Six Sigma, and that wasn't a good thing.

George and his conclave of supervisors had made the strategic decision to stay with the old mixer and the queue rather than use the newer mixer and try to figure out how to separate the good material from the bad. They also figured out that any extra capacity they gained would be lost while they queued up in front of the inspection process; not to mention what they lost to scrap.

I didn't want to make George feel any worse than he already did by trying to enlighten him to the fact that 100 percent inspection was not inspection. 100 percent inspection is sorting, so I bit my tongue.

Instead I questioned George "Do you really think the issue is trying to squeeze extra capacity out of this machine, or is the problem really the inherent capability?" I continued before he answered, "Would it be easier to take a machine, which has the ability to produce an adequate amount of material and focus on improving the capability?"

George replied as I hoped he would, "I never really thought of it that way." He ended his thought by saying, "We usually just do inspection."

Leaning Into Six Sigma

The power of asking simple, open-ended questions never ceases to amaze me. I always see managers pushing their people to 'think out of the box.' Of course this always seems like a wise thing to say, but lately I've realized it was the people who used that saying that are usually incapable of 'thinking outside the box.' To hide this deficiency, they encourage others to do it. Unfortunately these enlightened managers have no idea how to help their employees do it.

It takes good questions. Asking different questions will lead them out of the box, and aren't they supposed to be leaders? Maybe they didn't know how to figure out what the questions should be. It was an interesting point to pontificate but I had a mixer to work on. So I chuckled to myself, hoping that no one was paying attention to me, and thought, *"Man I love this stuff!"*

As I approached the mixer, it was apparent that the 5S fairy had dropped by. Things were clean, organized, and labeled. Good start. Some of the noise was out of the system. Processes were documented. There goes another piece of the variation. It looked like George was serious about the 5S and Work Standardization. It appeared he had taken over ownership. I was impressed.

The work that had been done was a good first step towards institutionalization of the two initiatives. It wasn't 'that guy's' program any more. It was becoming George's process for solving chronic organizational issues. When it transitioned to the way SG does business, then we would really be making progress.

It seems this was my day for introspection. I kept catching myself thinking of different discussions I had participated in over the past few months. One of the comments that really stuck in my mind from the war stories was how consultants had been hired to make changes, and the changes reverted back when the consultant left. Of course this would happen. It is an issue of ownership. If the consultant is the only one who owns the program, of course it would leave when they did.

The reason Motorola, Allied Signal and General Electric were so good was that they were learning organizations. They overcame inertia. They accepted programs without whining about "the program of the day." They embraced it, modified it to fit their culture, and then owned it.

But I digress... back to the issue at hand. I knew I could probably solve the problem George was facing in a couple of days by myself, but then it would be *my* solution. In order for this process to be meaningful, I needed to make the solution belong to George and his team. They had to walk away from the situation believing that the next time something like this surfaced, they would be equipped to handle it. Successfully.

Before getting in too deep with all the players as a team, I decided I wanted to get "up to speed" on the process as it was actually performed. I began with the older mixer first, mixer #1. The newer mixer was mixer #2, (obviously this numbering scheme was set up by someone who was very right brained - NOT). I began to draw a simple process map on a piece of paper, blocking out the steps and identifying the various materials.

The tools and materials were sitting around the machine as inputs. I also took some time to review the other documents and controls, which were easily accessible. The process map I sketched wasn't a thing of beauty, with all the correct symbols and notations, but it was accurate. By completing this rough high-level map, I could introduce it at the first team meeting to help get the group focused.

In a more traditional Black Belt project, such as I had worked with in the past, we would have taken the time to complete this task in a conference room with the team. By involving everyone in the operation, it tended to be a longer process, followed by hours on the computer to make it "look pretty." Maybe that was where the idea of Black Belt projects taking four to five months came from. Sure, the certification process took that long, but after certification the projects should be completed much more quickly.

It might be interesting to run a correlation study between time to completion of a project and the level of Champion involvement. Using the problem solving formula $Y = f(x)$, time would be a function of what? It can't be the tools. They only go as fast as the people who use them. But it is easier to blame the tools. When will we learn that focusing on blame isn't value added? For the time investment, I was not going to be any more effective, and I was time constrained. More importantly, George was time constrained. Efficiency was always the main issue.

After I captured all the steps I could observe on my map, I started a conversation with the mixer operator. He had been keeping an eye on me since my arrival, and to be honest, I should have gone over to introduce myself. But I didn't. That's pretty ironic, because I would normally slam a Black Belt if they rode into a project like this acting like the Lone Ranger. I rationalized my approach by thinking that since I'm not being trained here, I can do whatever I think I need to do.

I walked over to the operator, turns out his name is Doc.

Leaning Into Six Sigma

I showed him the pages I was working on, and began explaining what I had been drawing. I also asked him what he thought of my work. He studied the drawing for a few moments and pointed out a few things I had missed.

During our discussion we talked about what George had asked me to do. Doc said it made sense to him, but that he knew for a fact that mixer #2 couldn't make the material correctly. I asked him if he had any idea why, and he said he had made suggestions before, but he was just an operator so nobody paid any attention to him. I thanked him for his input and asked if he would be interested in being part of the team to work out how to move the material to mixer #2.

Doc said he couldn't understand why I would ask him, since he had been ignored previously, but he had been talking with Michelle about the changes we made on her line, and he would give it a try. I told him I was interested in his input, since I really didn't know much about mixers and it would be nice to have someone with his years of experience to help me out.

The part I didn't tell him was that I knew the more senior operators were on first shift. I wanted to tap into his memory of the various things which had been done in the past. Tribal knowledge can be dangerous when taken in large doses, but it can also be helpful in determining where to go next, because you can better understand where you have been.

I returned to my makeshift conference room/office to begin to list categories of potential team members. George was listed by name as the process stakeholder since he would be the beneficiary of the project. The process supervisor would be a stakeholder also. I knew there were some positions which had to be represented; an off shift operator, the process engineer (since it was their process), maintenance department, and a materials person. These were the 'have to have people.' I would add the politically correct ones later.

Next, I headed to George's office to get some help with names. After George had given me the names of the people he felt were best qualified to work on this project, I returned to my work area again. As I looked at the list I decided it was a good starting point.

I usually worried when management made suggestions about who to put on a team like this. Their criterion is usually to recommend people they get along with. Managers typically wanted people who thought like them rather than the free thinkers who are usually the best paradigm breakers. The paradigm breakers usually live on the fringes of the factory subculture. Typically, they aren't the first to be suggested for these assignments. But this was George's project. He needed a solution. We would just have to wait and see.

The first order of business was a little politicking. I was headed for the supervisor's office so I could meet him and let him know what George had asked me to do. When I was done with him, the process engineer was next. It is always a good thing to take the time to talk to the stakeholders, managers, supervisors, and anyone else with a particularly fragile ego before you talk to anyone else on the team.

By the next day all the politicking was done and we held our first team meeting. I had drawn my process map on the board prior to beginning the session, and taken notes as the "technical resources" explained why what was drawn on the map wasn't the way they set the process up.

Leaning Into Six Sigma

Then the operators explained why what the engineers set up didn't work. Lots of phrases like "I think…" and "I feel…." but no data. Not even an offer to go get some data. In my role as a Black Belt, it frequently paid off to just listen rather than talk. The notes I was taking on the "as is" versus the "as planned" process would come in handy when we began to develop hypothesis about possible causes.

The team adjourned the meeting after assigning several people with action items. Our first order of business was to gather enough data to run a capability study. The entire team agreed that the most critical issue was to get the Measurement System Analysis (MSA) started.

Since all of our solutions would be based on data from the process it was important to believe in the data we collected. The discussion about MSA generated the typical response. The quality department and the process operators angrily explained that they had a calibration program. We ran through the usual story about how calibration was a measure of gauge accuracy, and not even a complete picture of that. GR&R determines precision, together calibration and GR&R are called MSA.

Through all the projects I had worked in the past, I knew that the process map and the MSA were two things we couldn't do without. I explained to George (who was growing impatient) and to the team that these tools were not optional. These tools lead to the solution. Without using them in the correct order, we could be scrambling for the answer for weeks, or even months, without ever finding an acceptable solution.

During the next few days we completed the process map, problem statement, objective and capability study. The data was all fed into a document called a Failure Modes and Effects Analysis (FMEA). The FMEA uses the product of Occurrence (Capability Study), Detection (Measurement System Analysis) and Severity (Test, Reliability and Field Failure data) rated on a 1 to 10 scale. The product is called a Risk Priority Number (RPN). The RPN's can be used to perform a Pareto Analysis and set priorities for the Analyze phase.

I had been through the various voting methodologies used in other problems. The FMEA is the only tool that attempts to remove some of the subjectivity, and synthesize the various inputs to provide an analysis with a higher level view of the process.

We were progressing through the tools when we received some bad news about the MSA. The elongation testing had an unacceptable score. In many situations this stops all progress on the project, because it means that our data is suspect. While this was bad news, I was somewhat relieved to realize that the team understood the importance of the MSA when I noticed their looks of frustration.

We did not have time to hold up the project while we fixed the gauge, nor did we have the financial resources to order a new gauge and retrain all the operators in the methodology of measuring our product. We made the decision to run multiple samples and use the averages of the samples for the gauge reading. I made sure that the team realized that ours wasn't a good solution for production, but it could be used to keep a project moving.

This method of measurement reduces the standard error of the mean by taking the square root of the sample size (n) as the denominator. Our temporary solution allowed us to get the project back on track. The team didn't pretend to understand all the statistics but they were comfortable enough with the explanation to move forward.

As I guided the team to the Analyze phase of the project, we had set up various parameters for testing. We knew there were some interactions between the various compounds. Interactions are the reason for mixing in a chemical process. Hypothesis testing is not a good tool to evaluate those process parameters.

The team, and some managers outside the project, also had theories about various suppliers that needed to be evaluated. This didn't surprise me, the supplier issue always comes up. It is usually much easier to point the finger at the supplier than to fix your own process. While the supplier rarely proves to be the root cause, the problem is that if you do not treat the supplier issues with equal seriousness, there are people who will refuse to move on in the problem solving process. You have to work all the issues.

The team asked the supplier quality group to look into the suggested supplier issues while we continued to focus on the internal capability problem.

We set up the tests and collected data, being cautious not to inflate sample sizes. Large sample sizes force the test to be too sensitive, and this excess sensitivity causes everything in the test to appear significant. First, the data collected from the process was analyzed for Normality. The team started to balk at the time it would take to perform this test until I showed them how fast the statistical software could complete the test. I also explained that unless we could be sure that our sample data was normal, we could not make any assumptions based on the mean or standard deviation of the data.

After we discovered that we did have normal data, we next performed Tests of Equal Variances, using tests and One Way ANOVA to evaluate the means. With the inputs to the process not showing any particular problems, it was safe to move to the Improve phase.

As we entered the Improve phase we had some confidence that we had identified the most influential variables. We next had to evaluate the variables using Design of Experiments (DOE). This is a tool that not only lets us evaluate the effects of the factors but also gives us the power to evaluate the effects of the interactions of the factors.

DOE is a technique, which lets us manipulate all the variables at the same time, rather than the classical approach where we held everything constant while only one input is manipulated at a time. Black Belts are heavily trained on the statistics behind Analysis of Variance (ANOVA, a DOE technique) but in truth, the software did everything that we had spent days learning. It sounded impressive, and I am sure it served the egos of the instructors, as they felt superior in explaining a sophisticated tool.

I chose not to take up valuable time for my client. I could posture with the best of them in a peer environment, but not at the cost of my customer's project. Stroking my own ego was a non-value added step since I was not the customer, and showing off how much I know wouldn't move George any closer to solving his problem.

The success of designed experiments was really a function of how well we had done in the Analyze phase and Planning for the Improve phase.

Leaning Into Six Sigma

The first step in running a successful DOE was to make sure we could measure the factors and the response variable. The response variable is the outcome of the factors, often called the Y of the process. Since this technique requires setting high and low values it is always helpful to use the information we learned in the Measure phase to make sure we can accurately separate the various levels of input.

It seems kind of basic, especially since we had used MSA just a week before, but it was still new to some. I guess changing behavior really did take time and effort, maybe $Y = f(x)$ applies to change efforts also.

As I make my DOE report notes here, it makes sense to warn you, I'm about to talk statistics. You may not be interested, so if you aren't read ahead. I'll make it as painless as possible but there are still numbers involved.

The next step is logistics. What materials do we need? What are the changes we need to make to the machine as we change from one group of factors to the next? (This is known as a treatment combination.) We designed the experiment with five factors (five inputs that had significant effect on our output characteristic of interest).

Since we were going to have five factors at two levels each there would be thirty-two treatment combinations. The team evaluated the cost of running 32 treatment combinations and spoke with our process experts. They were convinced that we would not see any three factor interactions in the process so we would do what was called a half fraction experiment. We would only run half the treatment combinations, but we would be able to understand the single factor effects (known as Main Effects). We would also be able to understand the two factor interactions known

82

as Second Order Interactions. This was what was referred to as a Resolution Five Design. The use of the half fraction design also allowed us to do all the treatment combinations twice, to replicate the experiment. This reduced the risk of some random effect creeping into the experiment and causing a factor to look differently than it should.

Once we had selected the design and sample size we understood how many treatment combinations there would be. If we understood changeover time, then we could calculate how long the experiment would take. It is important to understand this; because DOE's are intrusive, we will make scrap, and it will cost money. The treatment combinations are so prescriptive that the DOE must interfere with production. This was another reason we leveraged the Hypothesis testing in Analyze phase. It allowed us to enter the DOE planning process with a reasonable number of factors and minimal amount of interruption. The Hypothesis testing we had done in the Analyze phase allowed us to do evaluations without interrupting production.

As we planned the DOE, we also created data sheets for the test lab so they could record all of the data necessary to accurately evaluate the DOE. Besides the data sheet with designated spaces to record required data, there were also areas to write down comments. Anything the team felt might be important was also logged. It was better to record too much than to miss something. The team organized all this with very little input from me.

By this point George was getting excited about the possibilities he saw coming out of the experiment and spent most of his work days involved in the project. As preparations were coming to a close, we assigned certain people to just observe what was being done. They were to log anything unusual in the process. The day before the DOE was scheduled, we conducted a dry run of two treatment combinations. This practice allowed us to do two setups and run everyone through the requirements of their position twice. Everything went well, even though most of the team members were a little nervous. At the close of the day, Doc made the comment that he had never before felt so valuable to the organization.

We cleared up some minor issues with the people who would be involved the next day and moved forward. The next day we ran the DOE. It went relatively smoothly. We had the data in about six hour's time. The analysis took about ten minutes, using software that was designed to analyze designed experiments.

I decided to take some of the mystery out of the statistics and conduct the analysis with the team present. With the entire team in the room, we hooked a lap top computer to an LCD projector and began pointing and clicking. Just to catch everyone's attention right away and not play the game of trying to make it look more complicated than it was, we did the Main Effects and Interaction Plots first. They provided basic information in a graphical format. The entire team could see in moments what we had found in the experiment. It was easy to see. Once we had discussed what each chart meant, we moved on to the ANOVA table.

OUCH!!! The team's reaction was as expected. Lots of numbers and acronyms that had a significant effect on most people's body language. I immediately began to explain what some of the numbers meant, and which ones were there for tradition and really didn't mean anything to what we needed to accomplish. The more columns of numbers I threw out, the more comfortable they became.

Our data said we had explained about 78 percent of the total variation. Two main effects and one interaction were significant. The interaction was with one main effect, which was significant, and one that was not. The next DOE would have to include all three of the factors.

Having weathered the ANOVA table storm, we moved to the residuals. This wasn't so bad. I could see the team building confidence around the numbers as I took the time to present the practical meaning behind each of the numerical outputs they were seeing. Additionally, graphical representations let us digest and comprehend the data without the statistical terrorist attack. The residuals told us we were in good shape. Normal and no patterns. We had most of the problem explained.

Time to zero in on the settings for our factors. Getting ready to do our second DOE was much easier. We knew the factors and the measurement systems were the same as they were in the first DOE. The only thing we were going to change was the level of the factors. We would move them in the direction that gave us the best response. With only three factors we could do a full factorial, which meant eight treatment combinations. With a replicate (repeat of the experiment), it was a total of sixteen.

We ran the DOE the following day in a little less time than we had spent the day before. The analysis was about the same, except a little lighter level of panic attack at the sight of the ANOVA table. It turns out we can get to where we want to go using blade design, speed, and the interaction of the two factors.

Leaning Into Six Sigma

Frequently this is where the Improve phase ends. But the team recognized that just running the DOE doesn't optimize the process. It only tells you what worked best for the factor levels you used. The next day would be optimization using Evolutionary Operation (EVOP), or Response Surface Methodology (RSM).

EVOP is a series of linked DOEs which are executed in a disciplined manner. The objective is to lead to the optimal point to run the process. After each iteration the team was assembled and they took part in deciding where the next levels would be set.

Doc was so jazzed by the process that he suggested we "push the envelope" and George agreed. "Let's not see what we would do under our current process knowledge constraints," he said. "Let's really start to understand what this process is capable of." In the end, the optimal spot was obvious to the most casual observer. Finally a solution, and mixer #2 was coming up.

The most difficult thing we were running into at this point was keeping every employee in the facility from "wandering by" while we were trying to have our team meetings. Michelle was more of a positive campaign leader than we ever imagined. She had been discussing our success with everyone in the plant and they all wanted to know when we were going to come help with their processes.

There were still a couple issues to resolve. As we brought mixer #2 into production, we ran the material into the main line. We circled back to the hypothesis testing from the Analyze phase and ran some Chi Square tests on the number of defects in old material versus new material, to decide if we had seen a significant difference in defect levels. The test indicated we were maintaining the same level of quality as we had always produced on mixer #1, but the new material was being produced on mixer #2. We would continue to work on optimizing the two processes later. The primary objective was to supply the same material we were supplying from mixer #1, only do it from mixer #2. The data showed we had achieved this goal. We were just about done. Yeah, I love this stuff.

The team walked through the 5S and Standardized Work steps again. Through the Standardized Work training, the team defined the new process as it had been documented and all the operators involved were trained on the new procedures.

Doc volunteered to assist in the training, which sent out a significant message to the rest of the operators. The team also followed up with the training department so that anyone new to the area would be mentored into the improved process correctly.

Since the Quality/Management system served as an infrastructure for the operation, the procedures were part of the document control system. The laboratory documents were changed as well. All the procedure changes meant these processes would be on the audit schedule for a while until it had established a record of compliance.

The process engineers had the job of programming the mixer so that many of the parameters were done automatically. This is a Lean tool called Mistake Proofing or Poke Yoke. It reduces the probability of defects occurring by eliminating the opportunity for error.

Some control charts were put into place on those areas we could not mistake proof. Everyone understood that control charts require discipline. If everyone didn't intend to comply with maintaining the charts, and more importantly, with shutting down the process when it was out of control, then there was no reason to post the charts. Everyone agreed to proceed with control charting as a measure of improvement in the process.

The next issue was to determine who would create the charts? Quality Assurance already had a person who was responsible for doing this so the responsibility was added to their list. The team would be trained in the use and interpretation of control charts so they would own that as well.

But the team didn't believe we were there yet, there was still one more thing to be done. I was voted as being the responsible person for this last task. I called Celia and requested that the team be put on the agenda for Sid's staff meeting so they could present their accomplishments. I was working with the team to create a ten minute presentation. This was how Black Belts were taught to present their results, and this team had certainly completed a Black Belt project.

The logic behind the ten minute presentation was fairly simple. Most managers are Type A personalities. They can sit about ten minutes before they feel like they have to jump in and take control of the presentation. The team's job was to transfer as much information to the staff as possible before the staff attempted to take over. The team was in control, things looked good, the process was running well, and the presentation was ready.

I showed up with the team and we waited patiently outside Sid's conference room door until it was our chance to go in. The door opened and we were ushered in. While the team was loading its presentation on a computer/projector, one of Sid's staff got up from his chair.

One of the team members whispered to me "Look, there goes our Controller. He thinks he is above this type of presentation."

As he was walking out of the room the Controller bent to explain to Sid that we would have to excuse him, because he had something important he needed to do. I could immediately feel the flash of red drop from the top of my head to the tips of my toes, and I knew the telltale red color of my ears was giving me away. I was getting mad, not for myself but for my team. They deserved better than this.

Before I could react in a completely irrational manner to such a blatant display of self-absorption by this arrogant so and so, Sid asked him what was so important that he could not spare ten or fifteen minutes to hear what a team had done to save several hundred thousand dollars for the company? Sid went on to explain that he considered attending reviews such as this a major function of his staff.

I smiled and my color dropped about a dozen shades as I settled into my seat. Looks like that discussion with Sid on "Visible Leadership" a while back had paid off. It had at least saved me the embarrassment of being escorted from the building for jumping across the table and assaulting this arrogant guy.

I had always been told "someone is sitting in the shade of a tree today because somebody planted a tree twenty years ago." I was certainly glad I planted that tree in Sid's yard.

Sid's message was clear as all his staff members adjusted their posture. It was equally clear to the team members of the mixing project that everyone in the room was paying full attention. There's nothing like a little brown-nosing behavior to enhance a career. The staff would just consider it the price of one more rung on the ladder. I was willing to live with the obsequious behavior until they figured out the difference between management and leadership.

The meeting went well. The team left completely empowered by what they had just been through. I remembered reading several things about the value of empowerment. There really isn't much written on how to do it. This process had worked pretty well. They had presented the program as one. No solos between Production, Engineering or Maintenance. They had witnessed Sid communicating his priorities. They probably wouldn't say it quite like that, but the result would be the same and they wanted to tell someone. The most important thing was they wanted to go fix something else.

I love this job, I love being "that guy."

Chapter Ten

A Moment of Discomfort

The day after the team's presentation to Sid and his staff, I ran into George in the hall. I didn't want to make a big deal out of the success we had both witnessed, but apparently George did. I glanced his way ready to give a polite "good day" and keep moving, but the urgency in George's eyes made me stop. My first thought was that he had another pressing problem that he didn't feel quite ready to handle. But George surprised me, again.

"Hi Sam," George said as he took my hand and shook it until I was sure that my arm was about to be dislodged. I took a half step back, and as I reached to massage my shoulder from the vicious hand shake, I was surprised to see the fifty dollar bill George had palmed into my hand.

"Sam, you won the bet, but I have decided that I want you out of here, and I want to sit down with you to discuss how we can make that happen."

I guess George couldn't stand the silence between us, because he didn't wait for me to respond, he just chuckled and continued to talk. "The mixer project was so successful that the staff has decided we want to incorporate Lean and

91

Leaning Into Six Sigma

Six Sigma into every process in our organization." George went on to explain by saying, "I have volunteered to be the first name on the roster for SG's initial wave of Black Belt training, and we want you to help get us through the process".

I accepted George's plan to lay out the transition from dependence to independence for SG with the understanding that my time in the organization would be spent transferring knowledge and working my way out. I glanced at George for a reaction and noticed he was smiling.

"Sure, I can't wait to take this through the entire plant."

Man, I *love* this job!

Chapter Eleven

Getting Organized to Get Me Out

The same afternoon that the mixer team presented to Sid's staff, I called Celia and asked if she could set up a meeting with Sid and George for tomorrow. I told her I knew they were very busy men but I felt it was important that we meet. Celia said she would arrange it. That meant it would happen. When she said she would do her best it was a coin toss. When she commits, the other two just need to surrender and show up. It's a done deal.

The meeting for tomorrow was critical in order to establish metrics for the organization. One of the things I was planning to explain to Sid was that time at the job didn't correlate to accomplishment on the job. If I could get the management group focused on the correct metrics, they would no longer waste time wondering who was working the longest hours. There was an engineering supervisor who even stood at the plant exit every day at the end of first shift and wrote down names of engineering staff who left after eight hours. I wondered every time I saw him standing there if he considered this value added, or non-value added work. It was actually amazing he considered it work at all. As long as there were people like him there would be people like me. Remember, those 'consultant guys.'

93

Leaning Into Six Sigma

The other reason I wanted to meet with Sid and George was that they had displayed some very good behaviors recently. Just like the team, it was important that they receive some positive reinforcement for the good things, in case they were having trouble figuring out the good from the bad. The project stuff is the most fun, particularly for a true plant rat like myself. The most important thing I could do for the operations people was not work projects, but try to guide the Leadership Team towards more productive behaviors.

The next morning I checked voice mail first thing. Celia had left me a message that the meeting I had requested was scheduled for noon. It would be a working lunch for Sid. If I wanted something to eat please let her know so she could arrange it. I decided if I was going to do the talking we would all be better served if I kept food out of my mouth.

I arrived at noon and Celia showed me in. I thanked her for arranging the meeting. Sid and George were unwrapping their lunches. Both thanked me for the work I had done with the team. I started to tell them that the invoice was in the accounting department, and Net 1 versus Net 30 would be sufficient thanks, but I bit my tongue.

Seems I'd done a lot of tongue biting lately. Yes, accounts receivable has a cycle time, and associated opportunity cost. I don't think any of these high powered business minds had trouble figuring that out. What was so difficult in extrapolating that concept to everything else? Why did they understand it for A/Rs and think it was a new concept to other transaction processes?

It was truly amazing that everyone struggled with applying these concepts outside of manufacturing. As one of "those guys," I have found that the only thing that all

94

Leaning Into Six Sigma

organizations have in common is their unyielding belief that they are *different!* This is the same autistic behavior documented by Dr. Deming a few decades ago. Talk about a long learning curve! Maybe that was another one of those "Resisting Change" behaviors. The truth of the matter is, the differences are negligible, and rather than wasting time finding differences, they should have been struggling with how they are alike.

I had observed over time that the white collar world believed these programs were geared toward manufacturing. Transactional processes, as they are known, were different. Since transactions were carried out in offices, they must be different. But again, I digress. I realized that it was time to focus on the meeting at hand.

Sid and George spent about ten minutes talking about how well the Lean and Six Sigma programs were going. They enjoyed the presentation yesterday because it had clearly demonstrated that if we had been focused on the defect level alone, the mixer would still not be an issue, and we still would not know it. I told them that the cutesy little saying about 'lowering the water to expose the rocks in the river' had become one of those inane sayings like 'working smarter' 'thinking outside of the box' and 'break paradigms' that were mouthed by people who had, for the most part, no clue what to do to correct a problem.

If you 'lower the water' (ie. safety stock and inventory) you have not only exposed the rocks (quality issues, downtime, set up and cycle time problems etc.), but in a very practical sense you have also exposed your customer. If you aren't prepared to deal with the rocks, using a process such as Six Sigma, then you had better cover them back up. The

95

thought of covering them back up is borderline insanity. It is expensive, inefficient, and counterproductive. It is, however, a better alternative than trying to plead your case to your customer, when you just shut them down, that you were just exposing the rocks. You will, most likely, not win any Supplier of the Year awards.

We spent the next half hour or so discussing the many things they had been doing which were helping to make the Lean and Six Sigma programs successful. They had had a couple of successes which they could publicize around the plant so people would understand what was going on. They had a good demonstration yesterday, which highlighted that it isn't an either/or situation.

I also explained that as management, their job is to lead the integration and drive the alignment with the company Vision and Mission Statements. I handed them a couple of pages I had created to help them understand what I was talking about.

As I reviewed the documents I had given them, I failed to recognize that they had no understanding of what I was trying to illustrate. Slightly amused with myself for being so dense, I paused and said, "Hey guys, why don't we spend some time reviewing what these individual pages are telling us."

Both George and Sid smiled and nodded gratefully. Neither wanted to be the one to say, "What the heck is this stuff?" But both were thinking just that.

The first page was the basic flow, which shows the links between several pieces of the initiative puzzle, and how they need to fit together. Sid and George both thought this was interesting, but it lacked detail. If they were going to implement this, they needed more detail. I explained how this was not meant to be a cookbook. The 'one size fits all' mentality was not appropriate here. The details for the deployment and integration should come from the Steering Committee. It is *that* detailed plan which allows them to understand when and where they can use a consultant. But more importantly, the work of the committee will help to control the time and involvement of that consultant, so SG doesn't wake up and find "that guy" still there ten years from now, with the implementation still not completed.

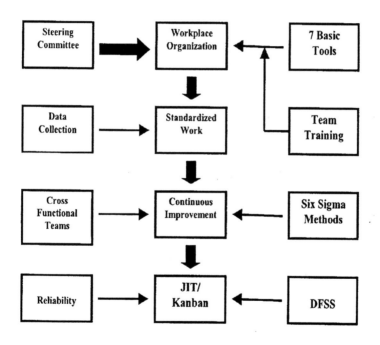

Basic Flow: Six Sigma/Lean Integration Model

Leaning Into Six Sigma

The next page of the handout provided the same structure, as far as being a block diagram, but this one covered the involvement of the Steering Committee. Before reviewing this next page, I did a sanity check with Sid and George to make sure we were all still on the same page (literally). Both said they weren't positive they had all the links, but they felt relatively comfortable continuing the discussion, so we moved on.

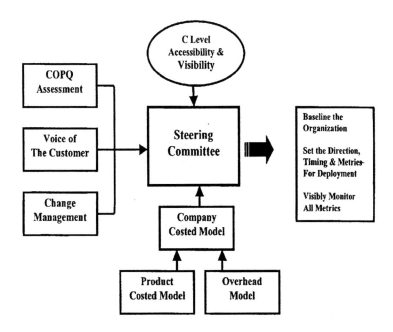

Steering Committee: Inputs and Outputs

They now understood that the Steering Committee had to have input from all areas of the business before they could produce the Baseline, Deployment Plan and Metrics. Surprisingly, Sid and George were on board when I explained that we were right back at the problem solving model $Y = f(x)$. The problem seems so much simpler when you just understand the relationship between dependent and independent variables. Effective change only happens when we understand the independent variables.

The next chart defined what would be necessary to implement a comprehensive Six Sigma program. Both Sid and George's eyes were beginning to glaze over. I told them not to worry, this stuff is always difficult to comprehend all at once. I suggested they introduce the idea at the next staff meeting and see what the reaction was. It would be Sid's job to orchestrate the overall strategy.

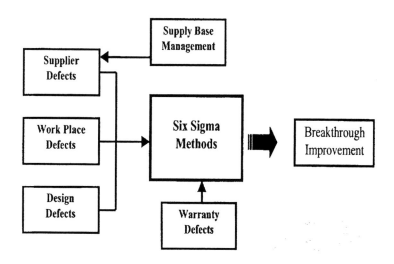

Six Sigma Basic Integration Model

I went on to explain that since George had already been the beneficiary of a lot of the improvement, he should be involved in selling the concept. Both shook their heads as if they understood. I knew they didn't, but they had been coachable up to this point. I believed they would follow through again. They had tasted success and wanted more.

We adjourned the meeting and I excused myself, leaving Sid and George pondering the charts I had just given them. My final recommendation for the meeting was to consider putting Michelle in the role of trainer for the program we were about to undertake.

One thing was sure. Both men understood that my main priority was to make them independent, and although they had a long way to go, they were on the right path.

On my way back to my work space, I stopped again and thanked Celia for setting up the meeting for me. I knew that with all the training ahead we would need her organizational talent to pull it off. Maintaining a cordial relationship with Celia wasn't a luxury, it was a necessity. Some things are never different between organizations.

Man, I love this job!

Leaning Into Six Sigma

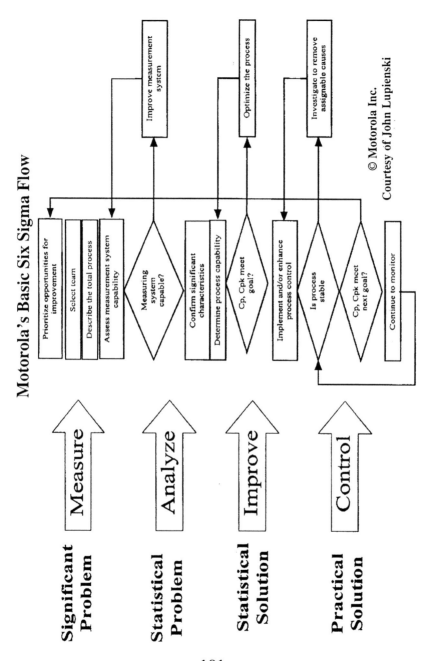

Motorola's Basic Six Sigma Flow

Improve measurement system

Optimize the process

Investigate to remove assignable causes

Prioritize opportunities for improvement

Select team

Describe the total process

Assess measurement system capability

Measuring system capable?

Confirm significant characteristics

Determine process capability

Cp, Cpk meet goal?

Implement and/or enhance process control

Is process stable

Cp, Cpk meet next goal?

Continue to monitor

Measure

Analyze

Improve

Control

Significant Problem

Statistical Problem

Statistical Solution

Practical Solution

© Motorola Inc.
Courtesy of John Lupienski

Leaning Into Six Sigma

Barbara Wheat is the Director of Six Sigma for Ingersoll-Rand Tool and Hoist Division, where she is currently bringing the tools and techniques of both Lean Enterprise and Six Sigma together to institutionalize a world class system of continuous improvement. Barbara has worked as a Master Black Belt since 1995 after being certified by Six Sigma International in an early wave at Allied Signal. Her latest position prior to joining Ingersoll-Rand was with Six Sigma Qualtec where she held the position of Senior Partner for more than 4 years. Barbara has successfully lead numerous companies through major deployments of Lean and Six Sigma throughout the world. Her e-mail address is BJW6Sigma@aol.com.

Chuck Mills has a MS degree in Production Operations from Texas Tech University, and is the President and founder of C.M. Consulting. Chuck is an independent instructor who has both taught and implemented Lean Enterprise tools and techniques to forward thinking organizations both in the United States and Europe. During the past seventeen years, he has assisted organizations such as Six Sigma Qualtec, Joe Auto, Inc., B.F.Phillips, Inc., Hershey Co., Lockheed Martin, Ingersol Dresser Pumps, Floserve, Chesterton, Owens Corning and others in continuous improvement deployments. His e-mail address is Cmmills@prodigy.net.

Mike Carnell is President of Six Sigma Applications, a Six Sigma training and consulting company established in 1995. This makes it one of the oldest and most experienced Six Sigma providers in existence today. He was also a founder and Co-President of Six Sigma International. Mike spent twelve years with Motorola, working in the Government Electronics Group and the Automotive Group. Since leaving Motorola, Mike has worked at Compaq Computer, Borg Warner, and Hi-Tech Manufacturing. In 1995 Mike was hired by Allied Signal Automotive, as a consultant for the Six Sigma deployment. Mike allied with other independent Six Sigma consultants, founding Six Sigma International (SSI). SSI deployments were launched at companies such as Siebe (Foxborough), GenCorp, Black and Decker, Navistar, Nokia, NEC, Libby Owens Ford, and Medtronics. SSI merged with Marshall Qualtec, to form Six Sigma Qualtec (SSQ). His e-mail address is SixSigmaAp@aol.com.